Alvin Fayette Lewis

A History of Education in Kentucky

Alvin Fayette Lewis

A History of Education in Kentucky

ISBN/EAN: 9783337160722

Printed in Europe, USA, Canada, Australia, Japan

Cover: Foto ©ninafisch / pixelio.de

More available books at **www.hansebooks.com**

A History of Education in Kentucky
by
A. F. Lewis, A.M.

Dissertation presented to the Board of University Studies of Johns Hopkins University for the degree of Ph.D.

Baltimore, Md. May, 2, 1899.

-----Contents-----

Chapter 1.
General Sketch.

Chapter 2.
Interesting Features of Early Education. A State University System. The Old Field Schools. Early Female Education.

Chapter 3.
Transylvania University.

Chapter 4.
Institutions more or less directly Connected with Transylvania University and other Colleges.

Chapter 5.
Other Male and Coeducational Institutions.

Chapter 6.
Female Colleges.

Chapter 7.
Professional Institutions.

Chapter 8.
Extinct Colleges of Some Importance.

Chapter 9.
The Public School System.

CHAPTER I.

Introduction. General Sketch.

Partly for convenience of treatment and partly because the periods are in a general way epoch making, the history of education in Kentucky may be divided into five periods, as follows:- (1) from the settlement of the State to 1820; (2) from 1820 to 1830; (3) from 1830 to 1850; (4) from 1850 to 1870; (5) from 1870 to the present time. It is to be constantly borne in mind however that the dates selected are only approximate, and not exact points of division, and that the movement, or movements, specially characterizing one period, as a rule, have their beginning in the previous one, and sometimes extend, at least in a modified form, through one or more subsequent ones. An attempt will be made here only to give the main characteristics of each of these periods, their most interesting individual features being reserved for more detailed treatment in connection with the history of the systems and institutions most closely associated with each of them.

The Period up to 1820.

The first thing that strikes our attention in the educational history of Kentucky is the early establishment of schools at its various stations, or settlements, notwithstanding the extremely unsettled condition of its affairs, and the great difficulties and dangers, especially from the Indians, which constantly beset its early inhabitants. The pioneers in the settlement of the

State were largely from the valley of Virginia, having entered Kentucky through Cumberland Gap, and were chiefly of Scotch-Irish descent. The leaders among them especially were men of more than the average intelligence and culture (1) and we see them early taking steps to promote the diffusion of useful knowledge among themselves and their descendants.

So the beginnings of education in the State are almost co-incident with its foundation. Within about a year after the first permanent settlement had been established at Harrodsburg in 1774, when it was yet uncertain ~~just~~ to whom the territory, now composing Kentucky belonged, as shown by the organization of the Transylvania Company, (2) we hear of a school being taught at Harrodsburg, probably in the Spring of 1776, by Mrs. Coomes, (3) the wife of one of the settlers, and that too, when Indians were skulking around the Station, ready at any moment to fall upon the unwary inhabitants. Some of Daniel Boone's companions had ~~just~~ been killed by them and their outrages had just driven

---

(1) Marshall says of the early settlers, (History of Ky.,vol.1, p.442,) "~~and~~ what may be assumed with great confidence, as a truth, is, that there were to be found in this population, as much talent, and intelligence, as fell to the lot, of any equal number of people, promiscuously taken, in either Europe or America." The "Kentucky Society for Promoting Useful Knowledge" existed as early as 1787, as is shown by a notice of one of its meetings in the Ky.Gazette of Dec.1,1787. The issue of Aug. 2, 1788, also contains a notice of a "Society for Improvement in Knowledge." A marked evidence of at least political acumen is to be found in the discussions of "The Political Club" which existed at Danville from 1786 to 1790, and independently entirely of all similar discussions, anticipated, in its debates, a number of amendments to the Constitution of the United States that were subsequently adopted. See "The Political Club" by Thomas Speed, Louisville, 1894.
(2) In regard to the character and organization of the Transylvania Company, see foot note to Chapter III,p. 30
(3) See Spalding's Sketches of the Early Catholic Missions of Ky., p.34; also, Collin's History of Ky., vol.I, p.486.

many prospective settlers back to Virginia. These are rather unusual circumstances for a school ~~to be taught~~ under, especially ~~by a~~ woman, but such were the surroundings of the first school taught in Kentucky.

Other similar schools were soon established, ~~as~~ that of John May at McAfee's Station in 1777, of Joseph Doniphan at Boonesboro in 1779, and of John McKinney at Lexington in 1780, within one year after the establishment of the town. The perils faced by these and other brave pioneers of education in Kentucky are illustrated by the fact that several of them were either killed by the Indians, or suffered bodily harm from wild animals. (1)

We do not know just who attended these early schools, or what was taught in them, but they were probably mainly intended for the younger children of the Stations where they were located and were ~~quite of an~~ elementary character. They were ~~the first~~ types of the early private and neighborhood schools, commonly called "Old-field," or "Hedge-row," schools, of which a more extended notice will be given later.

(1) John May was killed by the Indians in the early part of 1790 while going down the Ohio river in a boat, (Collins' History of Ky., vol.II, p.570). John McKinney was mangled by a wild-cat while teaching at Lexington in May 1783,(Collins' History of Ky., vol.II, p.226). John Filson, one of the teachers mentioned below, was killed by the Indians in the latter part of 1788 near Cincinnati, Ohio, of which he was one of the founders under the name of Losantiville,(Collins' History of Ky., vol.II, pp.432-433.)

Schools of a higher grade ~~however~~ soon appeared. John Filson, (1) the surveyor, adventurer, and first historian of Kentucky, as well as teacher, established a Seminary in Lexington in, or before, 1784. The pioneer Baptist preacher, Rev. Elija. Craig, established one at Georgetown early in 1788,(2) and, during the same year, the celebrated Dr. James Priestly took charge of Salem Academy (3) at Bardstown, (then called Bairdstown), which had been preceded there, as early as 1786, by a school taught by a Mr. Shackelford. This school, under Dr. Priestly's management, was for some time one of the most noted in the State, and in it many of the great public men of the early history of Kentucky received the principal part of their education.

The founding of private high schools continued steadily, in conjunction with another movement to be presently noticed, until Winterbotham, (4) in 1795, could truthfully say, in writing of Kentucky's educational facilities, "Schools are established in the several towns and in general, regularly and handsomely supported," ~~and~~ Marshall, (5) states, in referring in general to

(1) See reference to Filson's death above, as also Collins' History of Ky., vol.I, p.640, and vol.II, p.183; also The Life and Writings of John Filson, by R. T. Durrett, L L.D., Louisville, 1884.
(2) There is an advertisement of the early establishment of this school in the issue of the Ky. Gazette, (see chapter III, for description of this old newspaper) for Jan. 5, 1788.
(3) For the incorporation of this academy see Chapter II, p.31. The first advertisement of this school in the Ky. Gazette occurs on Nov. 29, 1788. Others occur later. For something of Dr. Priestly and the school of Mr. Shackelford, see Collins' History of Ky., vol.II, pp.35 and 200.
(4) United States of America and the West Indies, p.156.
(5) History of Ky., vol I, p.443.

the period we are now considering, "There are many educated and more means to be applied in that way than most other countries could afford. While a general propensity for giving and receiving literary instruction was obviously a prevailing sentiment throughout the country."

The other movement, just referred to, is the most striking feature of the State's early educational history, and is so interesting as to demand ~~of us~~, in another connection, a more extended treatment. It consisted in the inauguration of a system of local and State patronage of Secondary and Higher Education. Lexington soon after its establishment reserved land for Latin and English Schools and, by this inducement, as early as 1787, caused Mr. Isaac Wilson, late of Philadelphia College, as he describes himself in an advertisement in the Kentucky Gazette, (1) to open Lexington Grammar Schools; but State patronage of higher education came even earlier, as Transylvania Seminary, the first (2) "Public School," or Seminary of learning in the Mississippi Valley, of which we shall hear more later, was endowed by an Act of the Virginia Legislature in 1780 and further endowed and chartered in 1783, and other foundations and endow-

(1) In the issue of Jan.26, 1788, which says the school is again opened. The tuition in this school, as in most others of its class, was L4 per annum, (the pound being equivalent to $3.33), and advertisements state that good boarding could be obtained at from L8 to L9 per annum. The tuition was usually paid one-half in cash, the other in property, such as produce of various kinds, while board was paid altogether in property.

(2) For the antiquity of this school see Chapter III.

ments, by the mother State and by Kentucky herself, followed rapidly, until soon a State educational system was developed, quite unusual in its circumstances, and quite in advance of the ideas of the day elsewhere, in this country at least.

The main thing of interest in Kentucky's educational history, up to about 1820, is the development of this splendid system of higher education, composed, as projected, of a State University and at least one subsidiary Academy in each County, and probably intended to be supplemented later by a system of more elementary schools. The subsidiary academies were quite fully developed, and reached their culmination during this period, while Transylvania University was fairly inaugurated, and the foundations laid for the short but brilliant career upon which it was about to enter. The more elementary schools were however never connected with this system, and have only been established in any perfection in quite recent years, and then on an independent basis.

The main current of early public education in Kentucky began at the top and extended downwards. We have first the University or College and then the public school. This is not to be wondered at, as it was, as a rule, true in all the older States. A number of the prominent men among the early Kentucky settlers were themselves College men and among the founders of Colleges in Virginia. Naturally their first attempt to promote education in the new State, according to the prevailing ideas of the time, especially in Virginia from which most of them came, took shape in the form of an institution of higher learning. It was remarkable however that, in their hands, this institution should

have been planned to become the head of a great State system of public education, embracing even elementary schools---a conception in advance of public opinion at the time in this country at least.

Period from 1820 to 1830.

This period is marked by the downfall of the magnificently-conceived University system of which we have just been speaking. Even before 1820, the system of correlated academies had reached its culmination, and had, for various reasons, been acknowledged, in the way it was being conducted, as a failure by discerning public men. Soon after that date, the plan had been really abandoned as a State enterprise. The State academies did not however disappear at once but many of them continued as local high schools, and some of them after a time even developed into Colleges. Augusta, Georgetown, (1) and in fact many of the earlier Colleges of the State, were built upon old Academies, whose funds they inherited.

(1) Augusta was founded on Bracken Academy, and Georgetown on Rittenhouse Academy. In these cases the older academies were perhaps more prominent than in that of other Colleges, but Transylvania University grew out of Transylvania Seminary, and Centre College was, at least partially, based on Danville Academy, as was Southern College on Warren Seminary, while Louisville College was a development of Jefferson Seminary, and other Colleges were more or less directly connected with older Academies.

Public patronage, between 1820 and 1830, was confined almost exclusively to Transylvania University, which under Dr. Holley's administration, beginning in 1818, entered upon a peculiarly brilliant and successful era of its history, soon however to have its prospects blighted and its decline brought about by the unfortunate plan of its organization, and the state of public opinion, especially in regard to religious questions.

It is interesting to note that this institution was not, as in the case of many of the early colleges of the older States, founded by some church organization, mainly to prepare young men for the ministry, but that it was founded by the State, and was from the first considered a State institution, although never fully under direct State control, and its avowed purpose, as expressed in its first charter, was to prepare young men for the service of the State. The way in which it was managed however presents a curious blending of State and Church control, for it was also founded under Church auspices, and for the greater part of its history was under quasi-denominational management. This double management by Church and State to a considerable extent, at one time or another, extended throughout the whole of the early Kentucky university system, and, especially by the denominational jealousies it aroused, had a very disastrous effect. The ~~system's~~ plan of management, as will be noted later, was, ~~in other respects also~~, not such as to secure the greatest responsibility and the highest efficiency.

These things were largely instrumental in preventing the upbuilding of a grand system of public higher education, and in

causing the State to withdraw from her early policy of liberality toward ~~education~~. Kentucky was certainly quite liberal toward Transylvania Seminary and the early Academies, especially in the matter of the donation of public lands, and the exemption of these from taxation, as well as in her direct appropriations, although the latter were never large. The land grants were however not sufficient to make the system self-sustaining or to pledge the State to its further sustentation, while the control assumed and the responsibility required were not requisite to secure proper efficiency. When the original plan had thus been wrecked, we see the State so far reversing her original policy that, for a long time, she refused to make adequate provision for her public schools, and, even as late as 1865, without sufficient reasons, would not grant the appropriations needed to make the Congressional land grant of 1862 for Agricultural Colleges available for the highest educational uses, but left it to a denominational institution to make for her the most out of the limited endowment furnished by the general government.

Even during the period we are now considering, Transylvania University began to lose her hold upon the public good-will, and denominational colleges began to spring up, as so many centers of opposition, and to compete with the University for public patronage. Centre and St. Joseph's in 1819, St. Mary's in 1821, Augusta in 1822, Cumberland in 1826, and Georgetown in 1829, arose in rapid succession. Their competition was not greatly felt for a time, but was destined to grow to strong proportions in the succeeding period.

The failure of the Academy System did however cause public attention, even during this period, to be turned to the need of elementary schools, and public opinion was sufficiently aroused on the question to cause the Legislature of 1821 to appoint a Commission to investigate the subject and to report upon it to that body. This Commission, composed of Honorable William T. Barry, and other prominent public men, made, in 1822, an able report in favor of a system of public schools, and embodying excellent ideas in regard to how it could be inaugurated. The legislature was also induced to create a small 'literary fund' to support such a system, but nothing further was then accomplished.

Period 1830 to 1850.

Prior even to the beginning of this period, Transylvania University had been abandoned by the State in so far as the bestowal of public patronage was concerned, although nominal legislative control was still retained. The neglect of the State was however somewhat supplied by private and local munificence, and the University long remained eminently useful, especially through its professional departments, but it may be said to have now entered into a condition of gradual decline.

Several attempts were made during this time to resurrect its prowess under partial denominational control. Baptists, Episcopalians, Presbyterians, and lastly Methodists, were successively called to the aid of its waning fortunes, but, as a rule, with indifferent success, although the powerful church in-

fluence which Dr. Bascom was able to bring to its assistance for a time seemed to be going to revive the University's departed glories. When this too had to be withdrawn, in 1849, it sank even lower than before.

The peculiar feature of the period between 1830 and 1850 is the development, and further multiplication of denominational Colleges, a movement already begun in the previous period, partly in opposition to Transylvania University, and partly to supply needs which it could not then meet. It now became the settled policy of each imporatant denomination in the State to have its own representative institution. Several of these had already been founded but had not been strong competitors of the University, owing to their lack of funds and equipment. These were now strengthened and others established, so that most of the prominent denominational Colleges of the State may be said to date their existence, or their importance as educational factors, from this period. Centre, St. Joseph's and Augusta, especially, soon began to be well known and others, as Bacon and Shelby in 1836, were founded. This movement continued until Collins tells us in his Sketches (1) that, in 1847, Kentucky had more Colleges than any other State in the Union.

Special professional schools, especially of Medicine, also began to be established. The first of these to amount to anything was the Louisville Medical Institute, now the medical department of the University of Louisville, founded in 1837, as a direct competitor of the medical department of Transylvania University.

(1) Sketches of Ky., p.272.

The founding of denominational institutions and of special professional schools has continued through all the subsequent educational history of the State and has led to an unfortunate multiplicity of new and separate institutions whereas an enlargement of those already existing would have been far more preferable. One result has been that although the name has been frequently used, there has never been a real university in the State, even in the extensive use of the term, with all the usual departments and a complete faculty and equipment in each. Another result has been that the Colleges of the State have been quite insufficiently endowed. The State has never fully committed herself to the policy of sustaining a well-endowed University, while other institutions have become too numerous to receive large amounts from local and denominational beneficence which has been the source of almost all of the endowment of the various institutions. No single individual, either within or without the State, has given a large amount to any single institution and almost all that has been contributed has been given wholly by the people of the State, principally through the various religious denominations. Various communities have contributed with great liberality to institutions located in their midst without regard to denominational connections, and Presbyterians, Baptists, Methodists, Christians and other denominations have done nobly for their respective institutions, but local demand or denominational jealousy has called into existence a multitude of Colleges, each of whose share in the general bounty has been necessarily small among a people generally well-to-do

but not wealthy. The funds received have usually only been sufficient to give them a fairly good building and equipment, but have left them no endowment. So they have had to struggle on the best they could, mainly supported by tuition fees, many of the older institutions of the State having been, during the greater part of their history, rich only in the spirit of devotion to sound learning.

The fact that Kentucky Colleges have been so largely unendowed mainly accounts for the many ups and downs in their history. As long as local and denominational influence and their own good work have kept their halls filled with students they have had fair success, but when, for any reason, the number of their students has declined, they have declined in like manner, and the history of the State is strewn with the wrecks of educational enterprises. Cumberland, Shelby, Eminence, and others are so many examples of a chequered career, ending finally in dissolution.

Lack of endowment and strong competition have also compelled most of the Colleges to do a great deal of what is really preparatory and not college work, which has hampered their usefulness and, necessarily, to a considerable extent, vitiated their standard. This we will see applies especially to the Female Colleges of the State, which have mainly arisen in the period succeeding the one we are now considering, and for whose multiplicity we shall see there have been special reasons.

The period of which we are now speaking also witnesses the first inception of a State public School system. The law of

1838 established this, in a rather imperfect form it is true, but gave to it, what was a great gain, a regular organization. Its operations were greatly hindered, for some time, by the smallness of the 'literary fund' upon which it was based, and by the fact that this fund was not properly husbanded; but the system made really substantial progress during this time in the crystalization of public opinion in its favor, and, especially, in the fact that the 'literary fund', by the third constitution of the State which went into effect in 1850, was inviolably devoted to public school education.

Period from 1850 to 1870.

This era is noticeable for an unsuccessful attempt, made in 1856, to revive Transylvania University, as a State institution, in the form of a State Normal School, a much needed addition to the public school system. After a short trial of two years, owing to the lack of proper public support, this effort had to be abandoned, and the history of the University, as in any sense a State Institution, was ended. After this it sank into a school of merely secondary rank.

Again, an attempt was made, in 1865, to build on its ruins a great University in the name of the State, but really under what was denominational, but not intended to be sectarian, control. This plan was splendidly devised and seemed for a time likely to succeed, but it too was doomed to be wrecked, mainly by sectarian jealousy without and within. So Kentucky University, instead of becoming what it promised to be, an institution overshadowing all others in the State, was forced to take the

position simply of one of the principal colleges of the State.

Special professional schools have, during this and the subsequent period, continued to increase in numbers, especially at Louisville, until that city, with its six medical colleges and other professional institutions, has become one of the largest centers of professional education in the country, ranking since 1890, second only to New York City in the number of its medical students.

The further multiplication of denominational institutions also continued ~~apace~~. Female Colleges, especially, whose numbers up to this time had been comparatively unimportant, were founded in rapid succession and soon became so numerous that almost every prominent denomination in the State had two or more representative institutions. In addition to these, many communities founded local institutions to supply their own needs, which as a rule unfortunately aspired to become colleges. This of course led to fierce competition and, in many cases, to unsound educational methods and practices.

The number of female colleges, particularly, which have been established in Kentucky since about 1850 has become almost legion, their multiplicity being due partly to the fact, as noted later, that girls were for a long time excluded from almost all the institutions of higher learning in the State, and partly from the fact, that in so far as it was deemed necessary for them to be educated at all, it was thought that their education should be more of an ornamental character, and otherwise of a different type from that pursued by boys. These circumstances, in conjunc-

tion with the inefficiency of the public school system for a long time, and the consequent demand of localities for institutions suited to their own peculiar needs, have caused a large number of female schools to spring up which unfortunately have in most cases been ambitious to be colleges, at least in name, and to confer diplomas, if not degrees. Almost every school for girls in the State either bears the name of College or claims to do college work, whereas the work done by most of them is really largely secondary and even to some extent primary. No attempt has been made in this monograph to give the history of all these schools. Only those have been treated a considerable part of whose work appears to be of Collegiate rank. As it has been found very difficult to apply any absolute line of demarcation, it is probable that a number of institutions have been omitted quite as worthy of notice perhaps as some of those treated, but in general the same line of division has been followed as that used of late in the Reports (1) of the United States Commissioner of Education.

In one respect particularly, a great educational advance was made in Kentucky between 1850 and 1870. The public school system may, in that period, be said to have first become firmly established in the hearts of the people of the State, largely through the efforts of State Superintendent Breckenridge in its behalf, and an educated public sentiment, aroused by him and

(1) These Reports class female colleges under division A., embracing a few institutions of the highest rank such as Wellesley and Vassar, and division B., which includes all others. All the female colleges of Ky. come under division B.

others, called forth the Act of 1869 which made public education really effective by granting it, by State taxation, a more ample revenue. The opening of the educational year of 1870 marks the practical establishment of an effective public school system in Kentucky.

Period Subsequent to 1870.

This is especially noted for the continual growth of a sound public opinion upon almost all educational questions.

An enlightened public sentiment has of late caused the State to return to her early liberal attitude towards public education and no just complaint can now be made in regard to the way she supports the one institution she still controls, the Agricultural and Mechanical College, or her public school system. All school property has lately been exempted from taxation, (1) and the State College now receives a liberal contribution in the form of a regular State tax, while the effectiveness of the public schools has been greatly increased by considerable additions to the 'literary fund,' and also by increasing the State tax levied for the support of the system. This attitude of the State is a characteristic feature of the present period, but is not the only one of interest.

A system of graded schools has also been established, by the aid of additional local taxation, in all the towns and cities of any size in the State. This largely supplies a pressing need for secondary instruction and also relieves the Colleges

(1) According to the provisions of the Constitution of 1891 as interpreted by a recent decision of the Court of Appeals.

of the necessity of maintaining at least such large preparatory departments as formerly.

Most of the Colleges moreover have largely added to their endowments within the past few years, through private and denominational gifts, so that several of them now have quite respectable endowments for the work they undertake.

Many of the Male Colleges have of late opened their doors to women as well. This has continued so far that co-education may now be said to be almost a generally accepted policy in the State. It has had at least one good effect in obviating the necessity of the further multiplication of Female Colleges.

Quite a contrary and hopeful movement has even taken place lately in the conversion of several of these Colleges into avowedly secondary schools and the founding of such schools in various communities where formerly the establishment of a College would have been attempted. The opening of the Vanderbilt Training School at Elkton, and of the various preparatory schools of Central University and Kentucky Wesleyan College are so many illustrations of this praiseworthy spirit. A commendable disposition has also been shown to stop the further founding of separate professional schools, as those lately established have been opened in conjunction with the older colleges and the older professional schools have shown a tendency to affiliate with established institutions for which they furnish professional departments, as was illustrated, in November 1897, when the Kentucky School of Medicine became the Medical Department of Kentucky University.

Several of the Colleges of Kentucky have always been noted for their attachment to sound scholarship. Fortunately these, as a rule, have been able to increase their endowments along with others. So while higher education in Kentucky is still considerably hampered by a too great multiplicity of Colleges and their consequent lack of ample endowments, yet its condition is one of greater hopefulness for the future. The needs of the public school system of the State will be more fully noticed in another connection, but it too may be truthfully said to be making favorable progress.

Chapter 2.

Some Interesting Features of Early Education.

A State University System.

This system, which has already been referred to as one of the striking features of the early educational history of Kentucky, may be said to have had its beginning in the act of the Virginia Assembly, of May 1780, endowing Transylvania Seminary. For while the plan had not then been originated and this school was soon to dedevelop into Transylvania University and become, in a sense, the head of the system after this transformation, yet it was at first intended to be of the same character as that afterwards taken by the other Seminaries, or academies, (these words are always synonymous in early Kentucky educational history), the first part of the general plan to be fully developed, and was the model for the others in its original conception and, especially, in the method of its endowment by the State.

The original endowment act of Transylvania Seminary seems largely to have been copied in all of the first at least of the later academy acts. This act, (1) for its spirit, if for nothing else, is worthy of being quoted at length. It reads as follows:

"Whereas it is represented to the general assembly, that there are certain lands within the County of Kentucky, formerly be-

(1) See references to this act in Chapter 3.

longing to British subjects, not yet sold under the law of escheats and forfeitures, which might at a future day be a valuable fund for the maintenance and education of youth, and it being the interest of this Commonwealth always to promote and encourage every design which may tend to the improvement of the mind and the diffusion useful knowledge, even among its remote citizens, whose situation a barbarous neighborhood and a savage intercourse might otherwise render unfriendly to science: Be it therefore enacted, that 8000 acres of land within the said County of Kentucky, late the property of Robert Mc. Kinsie, Henry Collins, and Alexander M'Kee, be, and the same are hereby vested in Wm. Fleming, Wm. Christian, John Todd, Stephen Trigg, Benj. Logan, John Floyd, John May, Levi Todd, John Cowan, George Meriwether, John Cobbs, George Thompson and Edmund Taylor, trustees, as a free donation from this Commonwealth for the purpose of a public school, or Seminary of learning, to be erected within the said County as soon as the circumstances of the County and the state of its funds will admit and for no other use or purpose whatsoever: ---------

. Thus was planned the first school in Kentucky established under State patronage, and one which, at the time of its establishment soon afterwards, was truly in a 'barbarous neighborhood' in so far as the proximity of Indian Warriors was concerned.

The need of such an institution and the plan of securing its endowment seem to have been first seen by the Rev. John Todd, a prominent Presbyterian minister of Louisa County Virginia, and his nephew, Col. John Todd, (1) then a representative from the County of Kentucky in the Virginia assembly. The advice and influence of the former coupled with the ability and efforts of the latter seem, mainly at least, to have induced the legislature to pass the act of endowment, an act in advance of Virginia's usual educational policy at that day and the more unusal as occurring in the midst of one of the most gloomy periods of the Revolution and one specially trying to her. The Todds are therefore to be given the very highest praise for the inception of the plan and their names should for all time to come be placed high on Kentucky's roll of honor.

Transylvania Seminary was further endowed and incorporated in May 1783, (2), owing, as we shall see, largely to the influence and efforts of Judge Caleb Wallace, when its endowment was exempted from taxation by the State, the latter being another feature of its

(1) For the connection of the Todds, and also of Judge Wallace, with the founding of this Seminary, see Foote's Sketches of Virginia, 2nd. Series, pp.47-48. Further references to Col. Todd are found in Chapter 3.
(2) References to this act are given in Chapter 3.

organization appearing in the general academy plan. These are the principal ways in which this Seminary may have influenced the founding of the academies and so its history will not be traced further in this connection.

The first of the academies, subsequently appearing as a part of the regular system, of which we hear is Salem academy, located at Bardstown, and incorporated by Virginia in 1788,(1). It does not seem, at that time, to have received any land endowment, though it did later from Kentucky herself, and seems for a time to have been a private or local classical high School. In this capacity we have seen(2) it obtained quite a reputation under the noted Dr. James Priestly as master. It was later incorporated into the general academy system. Indeed it seems that when this system had come into full operation schools of higher education, supported merely by private or local means, were generally forced by its competition either to become part of the system or to suspend operations.

The first acts of the Kentucky legislature on the subject of academies are the act of December 12,1794(3) incorporating Kentucky Academy at Pisgah, near Lexington, one soon after, of uncertain date (4) incorporating Bethel Academy in Jessamine Co. and a third, on

(1) Littell's Laws of Ky., vol.3, p.579.
(2) In chapter I, p.4, where references are given in regard to Dr. Priestly's connection with it.
(3) For this act see Chapter 3.
(4) A note in regard to this act is to be found in Chapter 7.

December 15,1795,(I) establishing Franklin Academy at Washington in Mason County. These acts were similar in scope to the Transylvania Seminary act of 1783,but gave no endowment of public land as that had done.

The first really important acts, connected with the academy system proper, are the two acts of Feb.10,1798, the first (2) of which reincorporated Bethel Academy, giving it the plan of management subsequently used for the later academies, the second (3) of which endowed Kentucky,Franklin,Salem,and Bethel academies and Lexington and Jefferson Seminaries, (the last two established by the act at Lexington and Louisville respectively), with 6000 acres of land each to be vested in cooptative boards of trustees,as provided for in the case of Bethel,and to be held free from taxes.

The Bethel act gave to the trustees "all powers and privileges that are enjoyed by trustees,governors,or visitors of any college or university within this state not herein limited or otherwise directed." The President of the academy was also required to be "a man of the most approved abilities in literature." As shown by

(I) Littell's Laws of Ky. ,vol. I,pp., 298.
(2) Toulmin's Acts of Ky. pp.,439-470 and Littell's Laws of Ky.,vol. 2,p.,174.
3 Toulmin's Acts of Ky.,pp.,470-472,. Littell's Laws of Ky., vol. 2,p. 107-109,and Bradford's Laws of Ky.,vol.I,pp.,100./02

various advertisments and notices in the Kentucky Gazette and elsewhere,"Latin,Greek,and the different branches of Science,"(I) were required to be taught in at least most of these academies, thus furnishing to their students the elements of a fairly good classical education, not much emphasis as a rule being put upon the sciences. The powers conferred upon the academies by their acts of incorporation were sufficient for their conversion into colleges, without any further change of charter,as actually occurred in some instances.

The second act of February 10, 1798 itself,and especially the sentiment of its latter part,should add imperishable renown both to its promoter and to the legislature that passed it. The last part of section 5,and sec.6,of the act read as follows:

"And whereas it is generally true,that people will be happiest whose laws are best,and best administered,and that laws will be

---

(I)From the advertisement of Lexington Grammar School on Jan.23, 1788.This and such advertisements as that of Rev. Mr.Craig,on Jan. 5,1788,which speaks of the teaching of "the Latin and Greek languages together with such branches of the sciences as are usually taught in public seminaries",indicate in a general way what was actually taught.The general act of incorporation of Dec.,22,1798 says, (Toulmins acts of Ky.,p.,474,)"It shall be left wholly in the discretion of the said several trustees what subjects shall be taught in these several academies,whether the English languages,writing,arithmetic, mathematics and geometry only, or the dead and foreign languages and the other sciences which are generally taught in other academies,or colleges in this Commonwealth."

wisely formed and honestly administered, in propotion as those who form and administer them are wise and honest, whence it becomes expedient for promoting the public happiness, that those persons whom nature hath endowed with genius and virtue, should be rendered, by liberal education, worthy to receive and able to guard the sacred deposit of the rights and liberties of their fellow citizens, and that, to aid and accelerate this most desirable purpose, must be one of the first duties of every wise government. (Sec.8)Be it therefore enacted, that all the lands within the bounds of this Commonwealth, on the south side of Cumberland river below Obey's River, which are now vacant and unappropriated, or on which there shall not be, at the passage of this act, any actual settler under the laws of this State, for the relief of settlers south of Green River, shall be and the same are hereby reserved by the General Assembly, to be appropriated, as they may hereafter from time to time think fit, to the use of seminaries of learning through out the different parts of this Commonwealth."

We certainly have here an epoch-making act, one which is in general on the model of the great ordinance of 1787, (in regard to the Northwest Territory), by which it may have been influenced, but its spirit seems rather to have been drawn from that of the old Virginia land grants to Transylvania Seminary. It is certainly a note-worthy thing, for the time, to see a state thus setting apart a

system of public secondary and higher education. This is certainly an important enunciation of principle but it was not simply to be a barren announcement of a theoretical attitude toward education in the future but was soon to bear substantial fruit.

Winchester Academy, in the town of the same name, was established and endowed, on the same plan and in the same way, by an act of Dec. 19, 1798, (1) and, on Dec. 22, 1798, were passed two acts, the first (2) in reference to Bourbon Academy, and the second (3) in reference to nineteen others, which, especially if taken in connection with an act of the same date incorporating Transylvania University, are the culmination and completion of all the previous Academy acts, contemplating as they do a grand State University system. They are really a continuation of the acts of the previous February which serve as preambles to them, but are of wider import and so more remarkable and epoch-making. The act establishing Transylvania University, occurring as it does on the same day, it certainly seems should be taken in close conjunction with them, all being parts of one general plan.

These acts endow as before, out of the reservation previously set aside, the twenty academies named with 8000 acres of land each

(1) Littell's Laws of Ky., vol. 2, p., 217.
(2) Littell's Laws of Ky., vol. 2, p., ?.
(3) Toulmin's Acts of Ky., pp., 473-475, and Littell's Laws of Ky., vol. 2, pp., 340-343.

and also confer on each board of trustees the right to raise by lottery, a very common practice in these days and one considered by the best people as legitimate,(I) $1000, to pay for locating the lands and other preliminary expenses. Section 3 of the second act establishes the general principle of granting a similar landed endowment by the State to Academies in each County, by conferring upon the several County courts, in the Counties having no academies, the right to a donation of 6000 acres of land each and does not even confine them to the Cumberland River reservation, but says they may locate their donation for academies that may be established on "any waste and unappropriated land".

The part of the charter of Transylvania University, to be taken in connection with this general academy act, is section 3, which, after stating that the seat of the University may be moved from Lexington by a vote of two thirds of the trustees, adds "and, on the concurrence of the same number, they may, from time to time, establish at the seat of the University or else where, one or more schools as nurseries of the said University."

(I) For instance, some of the most prominent citizens of the State were on Feb.4,1812, authorized to raise $4000 by lottery to complete a Church on the public square at Frankfort (Collin's History of Ky., vol. I, pp.26-27). Another example of the moral ideas of the time is given in a notice in the Ky.Gazette of Aug.20,1788, which offers to give whiskey for the erection of a Church.

Circumstances seem to indicate that this had reference to the academy plan established at the same time and that it was aimed to make Transylvania University the head of a splendid scheme of public higher education, consisting of a central State University with co-related preparatory academies in every County of the State-truly a noble conception, for the main credit of which Judge Caleb Wallace's biographer thinks he is undoubtedly entitled. If the act of Feb. 10, 1798 contains in its closing sections certain sentiments and provisions that reflect enduring lustre on the State of Kentucky, (2) it is certainly no great exageration to say, that the combined acts of Dec, 22, 1898 "established the most enlightened, practical and complete system of education that could at that time be witnessed in America or perhaps any where else in the civilized world" (3) and that there are no brighter pages in the statute books of Kentucky than those that record these acts.

As already indicated, no doubt the main influence in the passage of these acts was that of Judge Caleb Wallace, one of the early justices of the Supreme Court of Kentucky, While a resident of Virginia, he had been among the founders of what are now Hampden Sidney College and Washington and Lee University, (4) and, on coming to Ken-

(I) Rev. W. H. Whitsitt, D.D., LL.D., President of the Southern Baptist Theological Seminary, Louisville, Ky., title of the work, The Life and Times of Judge Caleb Wallace, Louisville, 1888.
(2) Whitsitt's Life and Times of Judge Wallace, p130.
(3) Ibid., p135.
(4) For Judge Wallace's Connection with these institutions, see Foote's Sketches of Virginia, Ist., series, pp., 393-397, 442-444, and 458.

tucky, had become a member of the board of trustees of Transylvania Seminary in 1783, when, as a member of the Virginia legislature from Kentucky, he secured its reendowment and first incorporation. He later became a trustee of Kentucky Academy and, in 1798, was laboring to build up the latter institution by securing for it an ample landed endowment. He was also one of the principal promoters of its union with Transylvania Seminary into Transylvania University and seems to be the one who conceived the magnificent university system of which we have just been speaking. We also have reason to believe that he contemplated the later addition to the system of public elementary schools which would, according to his ideas and those generally prevalent at the time, form the capstone of this beautiful educational structure. The part he played in the early educational history of Kentucky entitles his name to be placed even higher than that of the Todds among the State's benefactors, as he had ever a conceptions than they of the State's educational needs and of the means of supplying them. It can in no wise be ascribed to any fault of his that his splendid ideas were never fully realized. Yet such was unfortunately the case. This grand system, so auspiciously planned, was never to be put into operation as a whole, and, as such, developed in all its capabilities and s soon to be recognized as failure.

Other academies were rapidly established and that part of the system was in quite full operation for a time, the movement contin-

County academies had been established and endowed with from 2000 to 12000 acres of land each, usually with the former amount. Evidence of the lack of public interest in the system and its ill success, however soon began to appear in the frequent bills passed by the legislature allowing more time for the location of the academy lands and appointing new trustees where the old ones had resigned or acted improperly. A tendency to get more and more out from State control soon displayed itself on the part of the trustees by their greater rights in regard to the disposal of the land endowments, until finally by an act of January 28, 1815,(I) they were given the absolute right of disposing of all their lands provided only the funds were invested in stock of the Bank of Kentucky, the aim of the legislature in this case, it appears, being rather to bolster up the stock of the bank than to improve the condition of the seminaries.

Public utterances showing the lack of success of the system, soon began to appear. Gov. Slaughter, in his message of Dec. 3, 1817, says that the academy fund had proved inadequate to meet the "enlightened and liberal views of the legislature" and by Dec. 2, 1817 recognizes the academies as failures. We find the Committee of Education of the State Senate, in Oct. 1820, calling for additional help for the languishing Seminaries and Gov. Adair, in his message of Oct. 17, 1821, says the Seminary funds have been generally rendered in-
(I) Littell's Laws of Ky., vol. 5, pp. 133-134.

efficacious by negligence or indiscretion on the part of those to whose care the donations had been confided. The system had then for some time been practically abandoned as a State enterprise, the only further public patronage extended to it being an act of Jan. 41, 1818(I), making general the exemption from taxation of all seminaries of learning, and an act of Feb. 14, 1820, (2) giving all fines and forfeitures in the various counties to the respective Seminaries located within them. This aid was however not very considerable and was insufficient to arrest the decline which had in most cases already set in, few of the academies, as the commissioners of 1822 (3) inform us, being, in 1815, able to raise a fund sufficient to support good schools.

The reasons for the failure of the plan are not difficult to find and have already been indicated to some extent. They may be enumerated as follows:-

I, The idea was in advance of the public opinion of the time. The people were preoccupied with other matters, partly necessary, such as driving back the Indians, and providing for their own physical wants, but their leaders were largely engrossed in acquiring wealth

(I) Littell's Laws of Ky., vol., 5, p., 31.
(2) Littell and Swigert: Statutes of Ky., vol., I, p., 596.
(3) Report of the Commissioners appointed to collect information and prepare and report a system of Common Schools. p., 17.

in a prosperous and growing State and they themselves too often considered the clearing, the tobacco patch and the cornfield, the best schools for their children, as Mc. Murtrie (I) says, in reference to Jefferson Seminary,"the clamors of Plutus drowning the modest accents of the Muses". The legislature at this time seems to have considered the establishment of a State bank and the floating of its notes of vastly greater importance than the fostering of the academies. This lack of public sympathy for the movement would no doubt have been overcome if the more elementary schools had been added to it and the people had become attached to it by its being brought into more direct and intimate contact with them, but unfortunately the system was never sufficiently developed for this to be the case.

2, The endowments were in many cases insufficient to accomplish their purpose, not because most of the lands set apart were poor and wild lands of little value, although some of them were no doubt of this character, but because these lands were really not sufficient in amount to support such a system well, and moreover much of them, in order to the speedy establishment of the schools, had been pushed into the market too hastily and disposed of at a great sacrifice, as was to be the case later, probably in a less degree,

(I) Sketches of Louisville, p., 134.

with the Congressional land grant of 1862 for Agricultural Colleges.

3. The principle reason for the failure of the academies is to be found in the faults of the plan whereby their management was provided for and carried out. The trustees were self-perpetuating bodies and, as such, little responsible to public authority. Besides there was no adequate provision for calling them to account for their actions. Butler (1) calls them so many "promiscuous and irresponsible Trustees." This opened the way for the primary cause of failure, speculation with and squandering of the funds, sometimes innocently, but often deliberately and criminally. The endowments were at first well guarded by law, not more than one eighth of the land being allowed to be sold for incidental expenses and providing buildings and apparatus, but subsequently acts gave the trustees too much discretion in disposing of the lands and opened the way for the subsequent destruction of the endowment by incompetent or scheming men. It was too often the case that speculators bought the land and the money was all put in one costly building, unoccupied and useless, "a monument of the folly of its projectors". (2) Sometimes not even such a poor result was obtained from the endowment.

There was no general plan and no uniform means were adopted to secure the success of the whole system. Some few schools, through the wise management of their trustees, escaped the general wreck and

(1) History of Ky., p., 188.
(2) Prof. Chenault in Smith's History of Ky., p., 70.

retained their usefullness; some of them as Bracken and Rittenhous. academies and Jefferson Seminary (I) even becoming colleges afterwards. But the following, taking from Marshall,(2) writing in 1820 in reference to Kentucky Seminary at Frankfort, is, alas too often, the record of the others. "But being afflicted with the Country disease-multiplicity and bad government- it has languished and revived alternately-in the building erected for it- until it has neither acting trustee, teacher, or student, as it is believed."

While the academy plan, as a whole, was thus unfortunately a failure, yet it was not entirely so. Many of the schools long remained as important local educational factors and one good result almost invariably came from the plan of endowment. Most of forty seven Counties of the State were able to buy a lot and build on it a fairly good school building, where a teacher could be supported by tuition, and where many living near by were able to secure the elements of an education of which they would otherwise have been deprived. They were often able to pay at least a large part of their board and tuition in country produce, a thing they would not have been able to do elsewhere. Prof. Chenault (3) sums up the educational result of the experiment by saying that "many of our early lawyers, doctors, ministers, and other professional men obtained all

(I) See note to Chapter I,P.,9.
(2) History of Ky., vol., 2, p., 336.
(3) Smith's History of Ky., p., 397.

their education in the seminaries.

It is a great pity, both for the cause of Education in Ky. and elsewhere, that the great capabilities of this early educational system were never fully realized. Collins has considered it a safe assumption to estimate that the Seminary lands, under proper management, would have realized for each county an average permanent and productive School fund of at least $30000, in many cases very much more than this amount, truly a magnificent financial foundation for a State educational system. Its comparative failure does not detract from the high meed of praise due the originator of this great educational project whose abuses he could not well have forseen and which certainly had in it the very greatest and ~~grandest~~ possibilities.

-Bibliography-

A greater or less amount of information has been obtained from the following works in the preparation of this article:-

Sketches of Virginia by Rev. W. H. Foote, D. D., Philadelphia, Ist., Series, 1850, 2nd., Series, 1855.

A Historical Geographical and Philosophical View of the American United States and the West Indes by W. Winterbotham 4 Vols.,

London, 1795.

A Description of Kentucky by Harry Toulmi   1792.
(I) History of Ky., vol., I, p., 502.

File of the Kentucky Gazette, 1787-1830, (Old Newspaper preserved in the Lexington City Library).

A History of Kentucky by Humphrey Marshall, Ist., edition, I vol., Frankfort, 1812, 2nd., edition, 2 vols., Frankfort, 1824.

A History of Kentucky by Mann Butler, A. M. M. D., Ist., edition Louisville 1834, 2nd., edition, Louisville and Cincinnati 1830.

Sketches of Kentucky by Lewis Collins, Cincinnati and Maysville, 1847.

A History of Kentucky by T. S. Authur and W. H. Carpenter, Philadelphia, 1852.

A History of Kentucky by R. H. Collins, LL.D., 2 vols., Covington, 1874. (the largest and best of the histories of Ky.).

A History of Kentucky by N. S. Shaler, (American Commonwealth Series) Boston, 1885.

A History of Kentucky by Hon. Z. F. Smith, Louisville, 1886, especially valuable for the article on Education in Ky., by William Chenault, LL.D.).

A History of Kentucky by W. H. Perrin, J. H. Battle, and G. C. Kniffen, Louisville and Chicago, 1888, (mainly compiled from other histories but containing considerable new educational matter).

The Laws of Kentucky by John Bradford, Lexington, vol., I, 1799, vol., 2, 1807.

with Acts of Virginia in regard to Rents, Land Titles, and the
Encouragement of learning, by Harry Toulmins. Frankfort, 1802.
The Statutes of Kentucky, Comprehending also Laws of Virginia,
and Acts of Parliament now in force,by William Littell, Frankfort
5 vols., 1809-19.

A Digest of all the Laws of Kentucky, together with Virginia and
English Laws still in force, by William Littell and Jacob Swigert,
Frankfort, 1822.

Collections of Acts of the Legislature, published by order of the
two houses, from time to time.

Messages of the Governers of the State, published in the Journals
of the two Houses of the Legislature, from time to time.

~~Reports~~

Reports of Committees on Education of the two Houses, published
in like manner.

A History of Federal and State Aid to Higher Education by Frank
W. Blackmar, Ph.D., Washington, 1890.

The History of the Presbyterian Church in Kentucky, by Rev. Robert
Davidson, D.D., New York, 1847.

Early Catholic Missions in Kentucky, 1787-1827, by Rt., Rev. M.J. Spalding, Louisville, 1844.

The Life and Writing of John Filson by R. T. Durrett, LL.D., Louisville, 1884.

The Life and Times of Judge Caleb Wallace, by Rev., W. H. Whitsitt,

D.D.,LL.D., Louisville, 1888.

The Biographical Encyclopedia of Kentucky, published b.
J. M. Armstrong and Co., Cincinnati, 1878.

A History of Fayette County, Ky., by Robert Peter, M.D., edited
W.H. Perrin, Chicago, 1882.

Sketches of Louisville and its Environs, by H. McMurtrie, M.D., Louisville, 1819.

Report of the Commissioners appointed by the General Assembly to Collect Information and prepare and report a System of Common Schools, Frankfort, 1822.

Articles on Education in Kentucky b T. M. Goodnight, A.M., in the Southern School, Lexington from June 1,1893, to J ly 31,1894, (extend up to Feb. 1844.).

The American Journal of Education,(especially vols., 4 and 5), edited by W.Russell, 5 vols., Boston, 1826-30.

The American Annals of Education,(especially vol.,1), edited by W.C Woodbridge, 8 vols., Boston, 1831-38.

Barnards American Journal of Education, 16 vols., Hartford, 1855-3.

The "Old—Field" Schools:—

Existing at the same time with the Academies was a species of schools which are probably frequently met with elsewhere in the early history of the States, especially south of New England, but which had, in Kentucky, a somewhat characteristic development and a local color. They were for a long time, a considerable factor in her educational system, lasting, as they did, up to comparatively recent times and only being displaced by the present public school system in its later and more complete form. These facts entitle these schools, although not strictly lying within the scope of this monograph, to something more than a passing notice.

They were ordinarily denominated "Old-field" (I) schools and were the kind of schools mainly existing, until the last generation, in the more remote agricultural districts of the State where access to the academies, which were located in the towns, was difficult. They were long the only means of education available to a large part of the rural population, they and the academies constituting the two principal streams of education in the early history of the

(I) The name probably arose from the fact that the school-houses were usually built in some old clearing, often a spot formerly occupied by the Indians for agricultural purposes. The term Hedge-row is applied to them by Prof. Shaler, (History of Ky., p. 139.), but the writer has never seen the term used elsewhere in reference to them, nor has he ever heard it used in Western Kentucky where the name "Old field" is frequently used by elderly people.

State. As we have seen, the very earliest schools of the State, as those of Mrs. Coomes at Harrodsburg in 1776, of May at Mafee's in 1777, of Doniphan at Boonesboro in 1779, and of Mc.Kinney at Lexington in 1780, the four schools antedating Transylvania Seminary, were all probably of this type.

As soon as a community were fairly settled, one of the first things they undertook was the building of a school-house, also usually a church, partly by joint subscription, but mainly by joint labor, to meet their educational as well as spiritual needs. These school-houses, especially in early days, were of the most primitive pattern. They were built of logs usually unhewn, the cracks being at most, only half chinked, with stack chimneys, and (I) clapboard doors and windows, the latter, as a rule, being without frames or panes, although greased paper was sometimes used in lieu of glass. There was often no floor at all, except the earth, and, if there was, it was made of rude puncheons,-split logs with the hewn side turned up. The only desks to be had were the same rude puncheons, fixed in various ways with legs inserted in auger holes or otherwise, at the proper height for sitting and writing, and without, as a rule, any backs of any kind to them. The only really comfortable thing about the whole structure, in winter, was the glow of the great fireplace where huge logs were generously heaped, and in summer, the breezes which circulated almost unhindered through the poorly chink-

(I) A name applied to a rough Chimney built of logs and daubed with mud.

ed cracks.

In this rude educational home, a teacher was installed and supported, as far as it could be called support, by the prorata subscriptions of the farmers of th neighborhood, a common rate of tuition being one 1£,7s., a year per pupil. The tuition fees were mostly paid in such articles as tobacco-then a legal tender in Kentucky; bear bacon, buffalo steak, jerked venison, furs, pot metal, bar iron, linsey, hackled flax, young cattle, pork, corn or whiskey, usually not over one fourth of it being paid in money, a rare commodity on the then frontier.

Some of the teachers of these early schools, as Doniphan, were men of high standing, often following, for a great part of their time, the calling of a surveyor, then an honorable and lucrative o c, but most of them were not, the character of the teacher and the methods he used being often almost as primitive as the house he occupied. He was usually some elderly man, of that or an adjoining neighborhood, who was supposed to have some education, but whose main qualification for the position was often that he did not know how, or did not care, or have the energy, to do anything else, having probably failed in every thing else he had undertaken. Once was some stranger, a traveling Irishman, or Englishman, or a wandering Yankee, whose qualifications for the place were presumed from the fact that e had seen a good deal of the world.

wages were very low. When teaching however, they were required to take up early and turn out late, giving short recesses and noon intermissions, the idea being that they must earn their money. They were otherwise practically under no supervision, except such as the pupils chose to put upon them, and taught according to their own peculiar theories, temperaments, and habits. They were often as rough and passionate as they well could be, and liberal in the use of the rod, even knocking down impertinent pupils, while, on the other hand, some of them allowed the scholars to do as they pleased. All, as a general thing, had written rules, which were frequently read, and usually vigorously enforced, the pupils often dreading the frown and birch of the master more than the screams of the wild animals they sometimes heard on their way to and from the lonely school house.

The instruction given in the first of these schools consisted of reading, writing and ciphering to the Rule of Three. The teacher had to be an expert pen-maker, but his instruction in writing rarely extended beyond "Capitals and large joining hand." (I) Geography and arithmetic were taught orally, the former especially, often in doggerel verse, which was frequently sung in recitation and in studying the pupils who were not reciting, adding to the motonous uproar of the

later Webster's Spelling book and Murray's English Reader and Grammar were introduced. Afterwards more mathematics and some classical instruction were added to the course in many schools, thus materially enlarging the education offered.

As already remarked, practically the only supervision to which the teacher was subjected was exercised by the pupils. This was regulated by custom with which the patrons of the school never in any way interfered as long as it was at all in reason. It only concerned such things as 'treats', upon certain recognized occasions, the granting of holidays, and similar matters and was enforced by the larger boys of the school, who rode the teacher upon a rail, ducked him in some convenient spring or pond, or otherwise made things so unpleasant for him, that he was forced to yield. A very common practice was to 'turn him out' until he granted the desired concession. This is well illustrated by the following characteristic incident taken from an article by Col. R.T. Durrett in the Louisville Courier-Journal of April 2, 1881-

On the 28, of April 1809, the first show as the boys called it, occurred in Louisville. It was the exhibition of an elephant, and there was a general uprising in all the schools for a holiday. The Jefferson Seminary and the schools at the head of which were teachers conversant with the habits of the place, gave the boys holiday without trouble but there was a New England teacher, recently come to the charge of one of the log school-houses, who could not

understand why the boys were to be permitted to lay aside their
books a whole day to see an elephant. He would not grant the holiday
asked and the boys went to work in the usual way to make him yield.
On the morning of the 28th, the Yankee teacher, as they called him, came
to his school house and found the door well barred with benches,
fence rails and logs of wood and the boys all inside laughing at
his futile attempts to get in. They promptly told him the terms upon
which the fort would be surrendered, which were simply to give them
that day as a holiday, so they could go to see the elephant. The
teacher was indignant and not being able to get through the door,
climbed upon the roof, and attempted to descend the Chimney. For this
contingency the boys had prepared a pile of dry leaves, and when the
teachers legs appeared at the top of the chimney the leaves were
lighted in the fire-place. Down came the teacher, for having once
started he could not go back, and the flames scorched him and the
smoke smothered him so that he was the powerless autocrat of the
School and knight of the ferule. He gave the holiday and went home
to lay up for repairs, as the boys expressed it, and the boys went
to the show as if nobody had been either burnt or smoked."

  Such were the methods of discipline and of teaching in the
old-field schools, which, as has been said, were to be found in many
parts of Ky., until the last period of her educational history. In fact,
some, of somewhat similar type, in so far as school-houses at least

are concerned, are still to be found in the out-of-the-way parts of the State, but their methods are far in advance of the primitive ones we have just described which for several generations furnished to a large part of the agricultural population of the State the rudiments of an education, which they would otherwise have been unable to secure. They were of great service in their day and time, being for a long period practically the only schools accessible to many, especially to girls, whose education must otherwise have been almost entirely neglected.

-Bibliography-

Smith and Perrin, Battle and Kniffen's Histories of Ky.

Proceedings of the Crittenden County Institute, Marion, Ky., 1877.

A History of Russellville and Logan County, by A.C. Finley, Russellville 1878 and 1879.

Articles on Kentucky Education in the Louisville Courier-Journal, for Jan. 2, 9, 16, 23, and 30, 1881, by R.T. Durrett, LL.D.

Sketches of Montgomery County, by Richard Reid, Mt., Sterling, 1882.

Early Female Education.

It is an interesting fact that although the first teacher in Kentucky was a woman, there were for a long time few schools at all for girls in the State, and these usually of the most primitive and poorest kind. Girls were excluded entirely from the early academies and the only schools to which they had access with few exceptions, were of the "old-field" type just described. The educational advantages offered in these were very limited as a rule and the surroundings at least not calculated to be very refining. Prof. Chenault quoting from Felix Grundy, tells us[I] that the teachers of these early schools, which girls generally had to attend if they received any education at all, "were often destitute both of a knowledge of polite literature, and good manners."

For a considerable period, the only schools in the State, claiming to give girls an ordinary grammar-school education, were those of Rev. John Lyle, at Paris, and of Mrs. Keats, at Washington, Mason County. Our information in regard to these schools is very meagre and can be given in a few words-

Rev. Mr. Lyles School.

The Rev. John Lyle was one of the Presbyterian ministers prominant in the early history of Kentucky. We find him attempting to supply the great lack of educational facilities for girls, by opening, in

(I) Smith's History of Ky., p., 299.

1803, at Paris, the first (1) Female Seminary in the West, if not in the United States. Mr. Lyle appeared to advantage as a teacher, and soon had a flourishing school of some two hundred or more (2) pupils. He continued his school until 1809 or 1810, (3) when he is said (4) to have closed it because others connected with the enterprise refused to allow the Bible to be read publicly in the school. Mr. Lyle then went into the active work of the ministry in which he labored with success for many years afterwards. (5). His severing his connection with the school seems to have broken it up, as we do not hear of it any more.

Mrs. Keat's School.

The other female school in the State, at this period, which is also said (6) to be one of the most celebrated in the West at the time, was that taught by Mrs. Louisa Fitzherbert Keats and located

---

(1) Collins' History of Ky., vol., I, p., 2 .
(2) Collins' History of Ky., vol., I, p., 2 , says there were from 150 to 300 pupils while p., 483 of the same Work gives the number as from 150 to 200. Foote's Sketches of Va., Ist., series, p.554, says the school sometimes had more than 200 pupils.
(3) Collins', (vol., I, p., 483), says he declined to teach in 1809 while Sprague (Annals of the American Pulpit, vol., 4, p., 170), says he withdrew from the Seminary about 1810.
(4) By Foote and Sprague, as above.
(5) From Collins' and Sprague, as above, we learn he was born in Va. in 1779, was educated at Liberty Hall, (Now Washington and Lee University), and was licensed to preach in 1795. He came to Ky., as a Presbyterian Missionary in 1797 or 1798. His death occurred in 1825.
(6) Collins' History of Ky., vol., 2, p., 557.

at Washington, for some time, the most important town in Mason County. Here we are told, the daughters and wives of many of the distinguished men of the State were educated. The school was opened in 1807 and closed in 1812 we do not know for what reason.

Other Early Female Schools.

Just at the time of the closing of Mrs. Keats' school, Loretto Academy was opened in what is now Marion County, and was followed, in 1814, by Nazareth Academy in Nelson County. Not long afterwards, in 1825, Mrs. Tevis and her husband established Science Hill at Shelbyville. Four years earlier Lafayette Seminary had been founded at Lexington. This last school while having a considerable attendance and reputation for a time,(I) does not seem to have had an extended history. Loretto, Nazareth, and Science Hill were however long the principal seats of female education, not only in Kentucky but in the Southwest generally, and are still flourishing in their educational usefulness. They will, on this account, although a considerable part of their work is now to be classed as secondary and so lying outside the scope of this monograph, demand a more extended consideration at our hands in connection with the history of the Female Colleges of the State.

(I) An Annual Announcement of the Seminary for 1825 says it was visited by Lafayette on May 13, 1825. It then had 9 instructors and 135 pupils and in the previous four years had had altogether 360 pupils. It is said to furnish every facility "for making thorough and accomplished scholars."

-Bibliography-

Foote's Sketches of Va.,Ist.,Series.

Collins' Sketches of Ky.

Collins History of Ky.

Sketches of Paris and Bourbon County by G.R.Keller and J.M.McCann, Paris,1876.

The annals of the American Pulpit by Rev. W.B.Sprague,D.D.,LL.D., 9 vols.,NewYork,1859-1869.

2

Chapter 5.

Transylvania University.

Transylvania University was formed by the union of Transylvania Seminary and Kentucky Academy, the history of each of which we will trace separately until they are merged into the more general and larger institution, the University proper.

-Transylvania Seminary-

We have seen in connection with the investigation of the early State University System, that this school had its origin in the act of the Virginia Assembly of May 1780, for the conception and passage of which Rev. John Todd of Virginia and his nephew Col. John Todd of Kentucky are entitled to lasting credit and honor. This act, (I) which has been quoted at length in connection with the inauguration of the early academies, put the endowment of eight thousand acres of land in the hands of thirteen trustees, including Col. Todd himself and several other prominent men of Kentucky, then the Western frontier county of Virginia, and declared that the Seminary should be "erected within the said county as soon as the circumstances of the county and the state of its funds will admit."

No corporate powers were conferred on the trustees mentioned

(I) Toulmin's Acts of Ky., p.,482; Littell's Laws of Ky., vol., 3, p., 571 Hening's Statutes at large, vol., 10, p., 288.

and not even a name was given to the proposed school. No definite idea was probably entertained of its being opened at an early date, for Virginia was then in the midst of what was to her one of the most disturbing times of the Revolution, and Indian hostilities in Kentucky, while experiencing a temporary lull, were soon to break forth with such violence as to bear down in their course the founder Col. Todd(I) himself and other trustees and valuable friends of the enterprise. The matter was however not entirely lost sight of, as we find that, on July I, 1780, an inquest of escheat was held near Lexington, Daniel Boone so famous in the early annals of Kentucky being one of the jurors, and four thousand acres of the land given to the Seminary was condemned and appropriated to its uses. This land together with the remainder of the original donation which was condemned later, is described as "as good as any in the Country".

Nothing more seems to have been done until May 5, 1783, when

(I) Col. John Todd and Col. Stephen Trigg were killed in the disastrous battle of the Blue Licks, fought on Aug. 19, 178. Col. John Floyd was killed from ambush near Floyd's Station on Apr. 12, 1783. John May, another trustee, was also killed later in a boat on the Ohio River in the early part of 1790.

another act(I) was passed by the Virginia Assembly, largely at
least through the influence and efforts of Hon. Caleb Wallace,(2)
then a representative in that body from the County of Lincoln in
the District(3) of Kentucky and later one of the justices of its
Supreme Court when Kentucky became a State. Judge Wallace was perhaps
more thoroughly identified with the cause of education, at
least Higher Education, in Kentucky than any other one man before
or since his time. We have already noticed somewhat his connection
with the founding of Transylvania Seminary, and shall see him
later taking an equally prominent part in establishing its rival,
Kentucky Academy, and then in uniting the two into Transylvania
University.

The preamble of the act of 1783, after quoting the act of
1780 donating public land to the school, gives the reason for its
own enactment as follows:

"And where-as it hath been represented to this
general assembly that voluntary contributions might be obtained

---

(I) Toulmins Acts of Ky., pp.463-467;Littell's Laws of Ky.,
vol.3,pp.571-573;Henkings Statutes at Large,vol.xi, p.,283.
(2)See Whitsitt's Life and Times of Judge Caleb Wallace,especially
pp.122-135;also Bishop's History of the Church in Ky.for Forty
Years(containing the Memoirs of Rev David Rice)pp.92-97.
(3)Kentucky was at first a part of Fincastle Co.Va.It was first
made a separate Co.by an act going into operation on Dec.31,1776,
and by an act going into effect Nov.I,1780was called the District
of Ky.and was divided into the Counties of Jefferson,Fayette and
Lincoln. See Littell's Laws of Ky.,vol.I,p.328.

from individuals in aid of the public donation, were the number of said trustees now alive, and willing to act, increased, and such powers and privileges granted to them, by an act of incorporation, as are requisite for carrying into effect the intentions of the legislature in the said act more fully recited: "Be it therefore enacted," etc.-

The act goes on to name as trustees twenty-five men, the very most prominent in the district, including Judge Wallace and seven of the trustees under the former act. Their names are worthy of being mentioned on account of their prominence in other matters as well as those of education, embracing as they do future governors, generals, judges of Circuit and Supreme Courts, legislators, and prominent lawyers, physicians and ministers. They are as follows: William Fleming, William Christian, Benjamin Logan, John May, Levi Todd, John Cowan, Edmund Taylor, Thomas Marshall, Samuel MacDowell, John Bowman, George Rogers Clarke, John Campbell, Isaac Shelby, David Rice, John Edwards, Caleb Wallace, Walker Daniel, Isaac Cox, Robert Johnson, John Craig, John Mosby, James Speed, Christopher Greenup, John Crittenden and Willis Green.

The name Transylvania (I) is then for the first time given to the proposed Seminary, and it is granted twelve thousand acres (2) of other escheated lands in addition to the eight thousand acres already bestowed. The twenty thousand acres are also exempted from taxation and the teachers and students from militia duty. The trustees are made by the act a self-perpetuating body on the principle of cooptation and are given in general all the powers and privileges that are enjoyed by the visitors or governors of any College or university within the State. They are also given the right to confer by diploma, signed by the President and five of the trustees, the degree of Bachelor or Master of Art, upon all such students, if such there be, as the said trustees, with the concurrence of a majority of the professors, shall adjudge to have merited the honor of the Seminary, by their virtue and erudition; and at the same time confer any honorary degrees which, with the same advice, shall be

(I) This name, a classical synonym for "back woods", or frontier, was borrowed from the use of it by Col. Richard Henderson of N.C. and his followers who, in 1775, by the purchase from the Cherokees of the portion of the state between the Ky. and Cumberland rivers, attempted to set up an independent government in Ky. under the name of Transylvania, in defiance of the claims of Va. to which they soon had to submit. The use of the name for the school was in one way rather appropriate as its founder Col. Todd had been a representative in the temporary legislature organized by Col. Henderson at Boonesborough in May, 1775. Col. Todd had come to Ky. from Va. just prior to that date. Later, in the Spring of 1780, he was sent as a delegate from the County of Ky. to the Va. Assembly. See Morehead's Boonesborough Address pp. 34-35 and 79-81.
(2) Davidson tells us, (Presbyterian Church in Ky. p 259) that when Ky. became an independent State in 1792, she so modified her laws of escheat in order to encourage settlers that the Seminary was deprived of this 12,000 acres and was only left the original 8,000 acres.

adjudged to other gentlemen on account of merit. will observe
that we have here, under the name of a seminary, all the provisions
of a college charter, in fact this very charter with its powers and
privileges not materialy changed, as far as can be ascertained, was
the one under which a University was afterwards operated.
We have already seen that the Seminary, by reason of its plan of
endowment and its purposes, was looked upon as a State institution,
but it is also to be noted that most of its chief promoters were
Presbyterians, a denominatation, then and for some time afterwards,
largely predominant, as an intellectual factor at least, in Kentucky
affairs, and quite a large majority of its first active board of
trustees just mentioned above, were members of that Church and prominent in its councils. The Presbyterians   and   d
to the credit of insti   Hi   Educ   K.   .(I)
Transylvania Seminary, the first institution in the State, distinctively one of Higher Education, owed its origin to their initiative,
and was opened under their auspices. In purpose and name it was a
State institution, but in organization it was really Presbyterian
by reason of its cooptative board of trustees being largely of
that denomination. The bad results of this unfortunate union of
church and State will soon begin to appear.
The trustees met according to the requirements of the charter on

(I) See Davidson's Presbyterian Church in Ky., p.314 and sq.

Nov. 10, 1783 "at John Crow's Station near Danville," which town had lately been made the capital of the District (I) and was also at that time its intellectual center, and organized with Rev. David Rice, ordinarily called Father Rice, (2) the oldest and in some respects the most prominent Presbyterian minister of the western country, as chairman. Mr. Rice was born in Virginia in 1733, had graduated from Princeton College, N.J. in 1761 and had later studied theology under Rev. John Todd. He had already been among the founders of what is now Hampden Sidney College in his native State, and having come to Kentucky in the Spring of 1783, at once took a natural interest in the new educational enterprise just starting there. He remained connected with the Seminary board until July 18, 1787, during which time he took quite an active part in its affairs. We shall subsequently find him equally active in raising up its rival Kentucky Academy. His successor as chairman of the Seminary board was Judge Harry Innes (3) of the District Court who presided over its meetings for several years.

(I) By having been made the seat of the Supreme Court of the District in 1783.

(2) So called from his fatherly care over the infant Presbyterian churches in the State. At this time he was only about 50 years of age. For sketches of his life see Collins' History of Ky. Vol. I. p.460, and also Sprague's Annals of the American Pulpit, vol.3, p.248.

(3) Also spelled Innis, but this seems at least the preferable spelling.

As has been said above, the original grant, as quoted also in the charter 1783, required the school to be opened as soon as the condition of the county and state of its funds would admit. We have seen that the extremely unsettled state of affairs in the pioneer District was at first an insurmountable obstacle. It continued to be a hindrance for some time to come, but soon the second of the conditions was the greater difficulty of the two. No funds from the endowment lands were yet available and no other means were at hand to inaugurate the enterprise. Good lands were abundant and cheap in the District, just then fairly settling up, and the Seminary lands could consequently neither be sold for anything much nor be rented, or leased, in such a way as to bring in much immediate income. The policy of the trustees from the beginning was to lease(1) these lands for comparatively long periods at a low rate, trusting to the growth of the country to increase their value and consequent returns. All the board seem to have done at their first meeting was to elect a chairman and appoint a committee to solicit subscriptions of money or property for the enterprise. They recognized the imperative need of such a school in a young and rapidly growing community and so issued their call for aid in its early establishment.

There seems however not to have been much response to this call, and what few small subscriptions were received seem to have been mainly contributed by the trustees themselves. The time was not propitious for such an undertaking. The financial trouble and distress due to the close of the Revolution were augmented by troubles with the Indians, the contest then on being mainly that of tomahawk, scalping-knife, and rifle and not of intellectual growth or prowess. Moreover the attention of the people was necessarily largely absorbed in subduing the wilderness and making homes and a livelihood for themselves and their families. Land had to be cleared, roads opened, and other means of communication and civilization prepared.

At a meeting of the board held at Danville March 4, 1784, one of the few encouragements received at this period and quite an important acquisition, as such things were a great luxury in a frontier settlement where they were rare and hard to obtain owing to the imperfect facilities for transportation, came in the form of the gift of a small library and some philosophical apparatus from Rev. John Todd of Virginia who, although at such a great distance in that day, seems still to have kept a watchful eye over the interests of the infant institution, the original foundation of which he had encouraged, and who showed his spirit in such matters by making the donation, "as an encouragement to science." The difficulty of com-

munication at the time is well illustrated by the fact that although the trustees seem to have made early arrangements to have these articles transported as promptly as possible, they were not received in Kentucky until the Spring of 1789. Notwithstanding discouragements and the still unsettled state of the country, the trustees persevered and at a meeting held on Nov. 4, 1784 resolved to open a grammar-school "at or near the residence of Rev. David Rice"(I) the tuition being put at four pistoles (2) per year, payable quarterly, and a committee being appointed to provide a suitable person to teach under the direction of the chairman. This committee reported on May 26, 1785 (3) that the school had been conducted at the house of Rev. David Rice since the first of the previous Feb. by Rev. James Mitchell and that Mr. Mitchell had been then employed to teach another year. So February 1, 1785 is the natal day of Transylvania

(I) Records of the board of Trustees of Transylvania University.

(2) A pistole was a Spanish coin whose value was about $3.60. Kentucky was at this time more directly connected financially with New Orleans than the United States.

(3) This, and in fact all the other dates of the University's history up to 1818 unless otherwise specified, are taken from the records of the board of trustees. That the Committee reported on this day has caused Peter (Transylvania University p.28) to give it as the natal day of the institution and that the school was to be opened "at or near the residence of Rev. David Rice" has caused Davidson and others to make Mr. Rice its first teacher.

Seminary, and Rev. James Mitchell was its first teacher. He received the modest salary of Ł30 ($100) (I) a year. The school was taught in the house of Mr. Rice because no other suitable place it seems could be found for it.

Such were the humble beginnings of the first (2) literary institution west of the Alleghany Mountains, an institution which after a comparatively obscure history of a few years, was to blaze forth with sudden effulgence and to remain for two generations the brightest star of the western literary firmament. Morehead (3) thus describes its origin. "A seminary of learning in a 'barbarous neighborhood'— a wilderness still resonant with the warwhoop of the savage— chartered in the midst of great political convulsion-- organized at a frontier station---on the extreme verge of civilized society! Such were the auspices under which the first literary institution of Kentucky and the West was established."

(I) The pound in early days in Ky., was $3.33 1/3, a value which is to be always attached to it throughout this Monograph.

(2) The facts clearly establish at least the strong probability, if not the certainty, of the Seminary antedating Martin Academy which subsequently developed into Washington College and is claimed by Foote, (Sketches of N.C., p.311) to be the oldest school in the Mississippi valley. Foote says Martin Academy was incorporated in 1788, (Merriams Higher Education in Tennessee p.227) gives this date as 1783), and if, as is almost certainly the case, the school was not opened very long prior to its incorporation, if at all, as was true of practically all of these early schools, it could not antedate Transylvania. - Its founder Rev. Samuel Doak could not have come to Tenn. before 1780. It bore the name of College before Transylvania did that of University, but we have shown that the Transylvania Charter of 1783 was practically a University Charter and we shall see that the whole school was soon of the grade of Colleges of its day.

(3) Boonsboro address p. 81.

We have no information as to how many pupils at first attended the school, but there were probably not many. Those were stirring times politically at Danville where a number of the conventions (I) looking toward the separation of Ky. from Va. were held during the time of the location of the seminary there. Courage and fidelity were also there required of both teacher and pupils, in staying at their posts, when the warwhoop of the Indians was liable to be heard at any time and rifles had to be carried to and from school for protection. Political and other similar matters seem, at least in that community, to have then had by far the largest share of public attention and the Seminary was left to struggle on with difficulty. Mr. Mitchell, of whom we know little, seems to have remained something over a year, and then to have returned to North Carolina from which State he had probably come. About the only definite information (2) we are able to obtain concerning him is that he married the daughter of the Rev. David Rice. After his departure, the existence of the Seminary was probably for two or three years only nominal, as no other teacher seems, during that time, to have been employed.

The trustees, if they had ever looked upon Danville as the permanent seat of the school, had soon, probably by reason of the lack of efficient local support in its behalf, changed their ideas

(I) Six of the nine conventions held for this purpose occurred between December 1784 and July 1788.

(2) Sprague's Annals of the American Pulpit, vol.3, p.248.

in this respect and had as early as May 26, 1785, begun to discuss its location elsewhere. A committee of the board on June 1, 1786 reported in favor of its being located on the Seminary lands, two and one-half miles south of Lexington. The legislature of Virginia, again appealed to in behalf of the struggling enterprise, passed an act on Dec. 13, 1787 (I) granting to the Seminary one-sixth of Surveyors' fees in the District of Kentucky which by a general law, together with a similar share of these fees throughout the State, had formerly been bestowed upon William and Mary College, an act which might have materially helped the school out of its financial troubles if its provisions had not been so defective as to make it practically imperative until an additional act of Dec. 20, 1790 (2) made it effective by attaching the proper penalties to its violation.

Meanwhile all efforts at endowment at Danville by private subscription had failed and the trustees having continued to

---

(I) Toulmin's Acts of Ky., p.136; Littell's Laws of Ky., vol.3, p.576.
(2) Toulmin's Acts of Ky., pp.136-137; Littell's Laws of Ky. vol. 3, pp.577-578, Davidson tells us, Presbyterian Church in Ky., p.289, that this law was repealed by Ky. in 1802. The writer has not been able to find any such repealing act in any of the early collections he has seen, but has found an act of June 23, 1792 (Acts of 1792-97, p.171) which suspended the act of 1790 for one legislative session. It is quite certain that the Seminary did not get the benefit of these surveyors' fees for very long nor was its income from them ever very large.

discuss the matter of location, finally, on April 17, 1788, resolved to hold their next stated meeting in Lexington, probably partly with the view, as has been noted, of soon locating the seminary on the endowment lands near there, and partly because they thought the school would receive a more favorable public consideration in that town. The celebrated John Filson(I) then teaching in Lexington took a considerable interest in the enterprise about this time, and through his articles in the Kentucky Gazette (2) and otherwise, was perhaps one influence in causing this action of the trustees. We accordingly find the board meeting in Lexington, Oct. 13, 1788, and without finally deciding the question of location which was discussed, resolving to open the school in that town, a convenient property to be rented until suitable buildings were erected on the Seminary lands or elsewhere. Two days later they appointed Elias Jones as 'Professor' in the Seminary at a salary of L100, payable quarterly from March 1, 1789, and made arrangements, if the number of pupils justified it, to have a Grammar Master at L60, and an

---

(I) See references to sketches of Filson's life in Chap. I, p.4.
(2) The Ky. Gazette was established in Lexington, Ky. by John Bradford and his brother Fielding Bradford on Aug.11, 1787 and was the second oldest newspaper published in the Missippi Valley being only antedated a few weeks by the Pittsburg Gazette. A number of bound volumes of the early numbers of the Ky. Gazette are now in the City Library of Lexington and furnish much valuable information on public affairs of the time in which its editor, John Bradford, took an able and prominent part.

Usher also, if needed. A subscription paper was at the same time drawn up to secure building funds. The response of the Lexington public does not seem however to have been at first much, if any, better than that of the people of Danville, and probably because the revenue from the leased lands, its only source of income at the time, was too small to pay his salary. Mr. Jones seems never to have taught at all in the school, as we find the trustees, on April 15, 1789, resolving to have only a Grammar-Master, assisted by an Usher, if there were more than fifteen pupils. The arrival at this time of the library and apparatus given by Rev. Mr. Todd seems to have been some encouragement and it was decided to open the school immediately at some convenient place. This convenient place does not seem to have been easy to find at first and an advertisement (1) for a teacher, inserted in the Kentucky Gazette, did not even receive a ready response. Mr. Isaac Wilson, who had been for some time the Master of Lexington Grammar-school, however soon applied in answer to the advertisement, and after being examined by a committee of the board, on May 22, 1789, was employed to teach for six months from June I, 1789 "at the public school house adjacent to the Presbyterian Meeting-House, near Lexington." (2) This building was probably the seat of the school of which Mr. Wilson had b...

some time master and the two schools were thus probably united for the time. Mr. Wilson's salary was to be at the rate of ₤100 per annum and the tuition rate in the Seminary was fixed at ₤3 per annum.

The new Master opened the school at the appointed date, June 1, 1789, which is the opening day of the school in Lexington. He went to work with a will, it seems, made a considerable success, at least locally, with the school, and on April 10, 1790 what may be called the first public College Commencement probably occurring in the Mississippi Valley, was held in Lexington. The following description of this commencement is taken from the Kentucky Gazette of April 26, 1790, "Friday, the 10 inst. was appointed for examination of the students of the Transylvania Seminary, by the Trustees. In the presence of a very respectable audience, several elegant Speeches were delivered by the boys, and in the evening a tragedy acted, and the whole concluded with a farce. The several masterly strokes of Eloquence throughout the performance obtained the general applause, and were acknowledged by an universal clap from all present. The good order and decorum observed throughout the whole, together with the rapid progress of the school in literature, reflects very great honor on the President."

The act of Dec. 20, 1790, besides granting to it the surveyors' fees, gave to the Seminary the use of the house it occupied free of rent, after Jan. 1, 1791, "so long as the public

shall have no use for the same."The needed subscriptions which had been solicited not being forth coming loans and even a lottery scheme (I) were resorted to in vain to supply a permanent home for the school. Mr. Wilson had been re-elected from time to time but the number of scholars, on April 13, 1791, was reported to have fallen from thirteen to five, probably largely on account of the Indian Wars then raging, and as these wars had greatly reduced the income from the surveyors' fees, the tuition was raised L3 to L4, at the same time Mr. Wilson severed his connection with the school.

On Sept. 1, 1791, Rev. James Moore, a Presbyterian clergyman lately come to the State from Va. succeeded Mr. Wilson as master. The latter probably reestablished Lexington Grammar-School, or Academy, in the house lately occupied by the Seminary, for we hear later of overtures from the Seminary Trustees looking towards its union with Lexington Academy and the Seminary seems never to have

---

(I) Although the writer has been able to find no such Act of Va., the records of the trustees show that a scheme of a lottery for raising L500 for the purpose of erecting a building for the Seminary was adopted by the board on Apr. 12, 1791,"pursuant to an act of the general assembly." There is an advertisement of this lottery in the Ky. Gazette of Apr.23, 1791, signed by a committee of seven of the trustees and containing the following expression of what would now be considered a singular blending of moral ideas. "Since the cultivation of the Moral Virtues of the heart as well as the advancement of the knowledge of the rising generation, is an object equally interesting to every good citizen, it is earnestly hoped that the scheme will attract the attention and Patronage of the public." A notice in the issue of April 21, 1792 says that the drawing of the first class of the lottery will take place on June 20, 1792. The amount realized from the plan does not seem to have been large.

occupied its former quarters again. Its Master, Rev. James Moore, undoubtedly conducted the school for some time in his own house, as is evidenced by certain allowances made to him on various occasions, by the trustees in the way of rent. Mr. Moor's salary the first term (I) was £25 and the tuition fees and the second term £38 and the tuition fees, he being allowed in each case to charge an extra fee for the Roman and Greek Classicks. The income from the surveyors fees and leased lands soon improved somewhat and the Seminary gradually became more prosperous under Mr. Moore whose salary was made 50 at the beginning of his second year. But the existence of the school was still some what precarious and its location still undecided until April 8, 1793 when the offer of the Transylvania Land Company was accepted and the institution permanently located in Lexington.

This Transylvania Land Company was composed of John Bradford and other prominent and public spirited citizens of the town, who having organized themselves in a corporate capacity shortly before that time, or March 7, 1793, purchased a lot (2) (now Goetz Park), upon which erected in course of brick house had been

(I) The College year for many years in the early history of Ky., was divided into two terms, one beginning in May, the other in Nov. April and October being vacation months. The stu......... in theselast two months.
(2) Known as lot no., 6.

previously erected, which, on Oct. 10, 1792, they offered to present to the Seminary on condition of its permanant location in Lexington. This offer was accepted by the trustees on April 8, 1793, when arrangements were made to make the house habitable for (1) the School. Lexington was then rapidly becoming the most important commercial point in the upper Mississippi valley,(2) a position it was to hold for some time to come, and was therefor a very favorable location for a college or university. The permanent location there of the Seminary which was soon to develop into a University, made the town for two generations the literary capital of the West, and helped it to hold the political supremacy of the state for a time. The organization of the Transylvania Land Company is the beginning of a policy of generously fostering the educational enterprises in its midst in which, as a rule, from that time forward, the town has never faltered. The members of the new Company especially took a great interest i the future welfare of the Seminary to whose board of trustees a number of them were soon

(1) From the nature of the articles purchased for this purpose, which were locks, hinges, glass ect., the house was evidently an old one, already on the lot when acquired by the Company and not a new one erected after the purchase of the lot by them, as is stated by several writers on the subject. Neither do the records show that the Seminary was required to pay for this building as is also frequently stated. The cost of the house is given as £400.
(2) Espy in his Tour in Ky. and Ind. in 1805, p. 8, says that its main street then had much the appearance of Market street in Phila. He adds that his brother who was there at Transylvania University, was making considerable proficiency in the dead languages and in general science.

elected, John Bradford becoming President of that body in 1793 and remaining so for many years.

Mr. Moore was continued at the head of the school which now at last had a settled home, and the greater prosperity of which, at least financially, is shown by the fact that, on Oct.10, 1793, the Master's salary was fixed at ₤100 per annum, and he was authorized to employ an Usher at ₤60 to teach the "Latin and Greek Classics," and an English teacher at a salary of ₤15 and the tuition in that department, which was fixed at 2₤,10s, the tuition in the Classical Department being ₤4. Arrangements were also made to admit, free of tuition, as many as ten orphan boys. The general condition of the institution is shown by the following advertisement taken from the Kentucky Gazette of December 6, 1793, the original spelling being retained:"The Transylvania Seminary is now well supplied with teachers of natural and moral philosophy, of the mathematics, and of the learned languages. An English teacher is also introduced into the Colledge who teaches Reading,Writing,Arithmetic and the English Grammar." The advertisement concluded with the following statement, "This Seminary is the best seat of education on the Western Waters;and it is to be hoped, the time is not far distant when even prejudice itself will not think it necessary to transport our youths to the Atlantic States, to compleat their education." John Price was the English teacher at this time but we are not

informed as to who the other teacher was besides Mr. Moore. The school had, however, hardly gotten settled in its new home and made a fair start towards prosperity when it experienced the first of the many troubles which we shall see it have to encounter on account of disagreement among the members of its self-perpetuating trustees, and the peculiar relation in which it stood to religious denominations, especially the Presbyterians. This denomination, through whose foresight and energy the school had mainly founded, were put much more on the defensive and were more sensitive than usual in regard to doctrinal matters on account of the prevalence at that time in Kentucky, especially among her public men(I), of the French Deistical philosophy of the day. This fact is to be constantly borne in mind in considering the attitude of the Presbyterians toward the Seminary. They had mainly founded the school but they never seemed, either now or afterwards, to have attempted to obtain exclusive denominational control over it which, by reason of their preponderance as an intellectual factor for a long time in the early history of the State, they could probably have been able to accomplish on more than one occasion by the aid of legislative action, as was done in regard to other schools by other denominations.(2) Their prominence in connection with the management and

(I) Several authorities agree that it was owing to the prevalence of these ideas probably, that Ministers of the Gospel were excluded from public offices under the first and second constitutions of Ky. a state of things they consider was very deleterious to the interests of education, specially public school education, in the State.(2) For instance in the case of Bethel Academy and the

administration of the school for some time seems to have been, on their part, more the natural result of their interest in such matters than of any direct intention to control it. It is probably true, as Davidson tells us, that they voluntarily retired from its board of trustees, and allowed prominent public men to be elected in their places in order to increase the popularity of the institution. It was doubtless in this way that they lost their numerical superiority in the board. They were satisfied with the school and were willing to patronize it as long as it conformed to their ideals of what such a school should be, but when its religious tone or teaching, by reason of other control, became what they considered dangerous, they simply withdrew their patronage and established one that better suited their ideas and aims, one of which was to prepare suitable ministers for the church; and yet they were willing to even take the initiative in coming back again when these difficulties were out of the way. They were also equally prompt to retire again and establish another rival when a similar emergency arose.

    Mr. Moore had for some reason,(I) which does not appear, become unsatisfactory as Master of the Seminary and on Feb. 5, 1794, Rev. Harry Toulmin, a prominent Baptist minister recently come to the State

---

(I) This was not probably, as some have stated, because of his leaning to the Presbyterian Church at this time on account of his trial sermon not having been sustained by Presbytery, for the Presbyterians later put him at the head of their own distinctive school, Kentucky Academy.

from Virginia, was proposed as his successor. Mr.Toulmin was a personal friend of Thomas Jefferson, by whom he was strongly recommended for the position. He also was a man of ability, and subsequently became Secretary of State under Gov.Garrard, but he was suspected of Unitarian sentiments and his friendship with Mr.Jefferson was not in his favor, especially in the eyes of the Presbyterians, as on that account he was supposed to be tinctured with French philosophy, or infidelity, as they considered it. His candidacy brought on a contest in the board, perhaps intensified by jealousy between the Baptists and Presbyterians, and although Mr.Toulmin was finally elected on April 7, 1793, the Presbyterian members were greatly dissatisfied with the situation and most of them resigned, either at once or soon after. Mr. Toulmin's salary per year was to be L100, one-half of the tuition fees and a residence. He was to take office on Oct. 9, following his election, but Mr. Moore resigned two days after that event and Mr. Toulmin was inducted into office on June 30, 1794. The Presbyterians determined at once to establish an institution more distinctively under their own control to which they could transfer their patronage. Their efforts resulted in the founding of Kentucky Academy, the history of which will mainly engage our attention until the two schools are subsequently united.

-Kentucky Academy-

This school we have seen, was established on account of the dissatisfaction of the Presbyterians with the management of Transylvania

Seminary, especially with the lection of Mr. Toulmin, as its Master. "Father Rice", Judge Wallace and others, prominent in founding Transylvania Seminary, were also leaders in establishing the new school.

The initial step in this enterprise and one that shows its purposes, was the issue by the

Presbytery of Transylvania on April 22nd, 1794, of an address to the
people of Kentucky, Cumberland and the Miami Settlement, proposing to
set on foot a grammar school and public Seminary, meaning by the latter
term, a department of collegiate grade, which was to be "under their
own patronage" and "might furnish the churches with able and faithful
ministers."(2) It was to be under the control of Presbetery in a general
way but was not to be otherwise sectarian. The charter of the school,
granted by the state legislature on Dec. 12th, 1794,(3) shows its spirit,
which is more catholic than sectarian, in the following provisions:
(Sec. 7), "The President of the said Academy shall be a minister of the
gospel, of the most approved abilities in literature, an acquaintance
with mankind, that may be obtained, and zealously engaged to promote the
interest of real and practical religion." (Sec. 15) "No endeavors
shall be used by the President, or other teachers, to influence the mind
of any student, to change his religious tenets, or to embrace those of
a different denomination, any further than is consistent with the general
belief of the gospel system and the practice of vital piety."

So, while not narrow in spirit, Kentucky Academy is the first school
in the state to be called denominational, soon to be one of the characteristic features of Kentucky's educational institutions, although it was
not strictly so, as it had no denominational name or legal church connection and was really, in organization, one of the state academies, the
first one chartered by Kentucky as an independent state.

(1) Cumberland was the country around Nashville, Tenn., then one of the
principal centres of population in that state. Miami referred to the
settlement on the Miami River, ocoupying a similar position in Ohio.

(2) Davidson's Presbyterian Church in Ky., p. 291.

(3) Littell's Laws of Ky., Vol. I, pp. 228-230.

Its charter conformed to the general academy plan with a co-optative board of eighteen trustees, its management as a somewhat distinctively Presbyterian institution being secured by having its trustees largely, if not entirely Presbyterians, Rev. David Rice, Judge Wallace, Rev. James Blythe, and others, prominent in local Presbyterian circles, being among their number. We shall see Bethel, another of the state academies founded about the same time, also soon coming under a similar denominational control for a time.

Presbytery, soon after issuing its address, appointed a committee of forty-seven, as canvassers for funds to inaugurate the proposed institution. These proceeded with vigor and soon raised mainly in Kentucky upwards of £1,000 ($3333), quite a respectable sum considering the time and the circumstances under which it was raised. In 1795, Revs. David Rice and James Blythe went East, as commissioners from Presbytery to the General Assembly of the Church at Philadelphia, and while there, appealed to a larger Presbyterian constituency and to general benevolence. They succeeded in obtaining in the Atlantic States, subscriptions amounting to about $10,000 (1) to aid in endowing the new educational enterprise. Among other prominent contributors for this object were George Washington, John Adams and Aaron Burr, the first two contributing $100 each and Burr, $50. (2) Washington, in connection with making his contribution, is said to have inquired very carefully in regard to the state of learning and literature in the West, as Kentucky was then called.

The first business meeting of the Academy trustees was held on March 11th, 1795, (3) when its location was decided upon and arrangements

(1) Davidson's Presbyterian Church in Ky. p. 164.

(2) This is as given by Davidson (Presbyterian Church in Ky. p. 124) and other authorities- Peter's Transylvania University p. 62 gives one of the original subscription papers which shows this sum to have been $40. It also shows that among other prominent men, Robert Morris gave $100.

made to erect the necessary building. The new school was located at Pisgah, seven miles south-west of Lexington, near the house of Judge Wallace and had as its initial endowment, as we have seen, about $14,000. Later, on Sept. 15th, 1797, it received a small but valuable library and some philosophical apparatus (1) amounting in all to about £80 in value, through Rev. Dr. Gordon of Loudon, contributed by himself and other English friends, and under the Academy act of Feb. 10th, 1798,(2) it was granted six thousand acres of land by the state.

Its grammar school department seems to have been opened on Oct. 26th, 1795,(3) and had, as its first teacher, Rev. Andrew Steele. On April 13th 1796, Mr. Steele was succeeded by Rev. James Moore, formerly Master, or Principal, of Transylvania Seminary. Mr. Moore was re-elected to his former position in Transylvania Seminary on Sept. 23rd, 1796 and notices in the Kentucky "Gazette" show that Mr. Steele again took charge of the Academy, John Thomson becoming his assistant on Oct. 6th, 1797, when the Seminary, or collegiate department, was first arranged to be opened. We know very little of the history of the school, but it seems in the main, tto have been fairly successful during the period of its existence. The last meeting of its trustees occurred in Oct. 1798, when the question of its union with Transylvania Seminary was finally decided and the arrangements looking towards that end completed.

Meanwhile Transylvania Seminary seems to have had somewhat of a similar history under Mr. Toulmin. The funds of the school seem for some reason to have become low again and so we find,that on the day he took

(1) Ranck and others mention certain antiquated pieces of apparatus now in Kentucky University as being probably parts of this old donation. They probably either belonged to it or to the apparatus given by Col. Todd, or perhaps to both.

(2) See reference to Toulmin and other authorities in Chapter II

(3) This is according to Bradford,(notes p. 438), and is probably correct. Davidson says the opening occurred early in 1795, soon after Presbyter. had issued its address.

the oath of office, the previous order of the trustees allowing free scholarships was revoked and but two teachers were employed during the administration, the assistant teacher for at least most of the time being Jesse Bledsoe, later one of the distinguished law professors of Transylvania University.

It is probably true that several of the state academies, especially Salem Academy at Bardstown, being in various ways situated under somewhat more favorable circumstances, were more highly prosperous about this time than either Transylvania University or Kentucky Academy. The people of most portions of the state, especially that around Lexington, then the commercial and for a time the political center of the state, were too deeply engrossed in the Indian wars of the north-west, the reform of the criminal statutes, the resolutions of 1798, the free navigation of the Mississippi river, the acquisition of Louisiana and similar matters, to pay very much attention to education. Later, the war of 1812 became a matter of all-absorbing interest, in which struggle we have accounts of teachers and scholars, especially in the "Oldfield" schools enlisting almost en masse.

Frequent calls for meetings, through the columns of the Kentucky Gazette, and the passage of a law by the legislature in 1795 (1) making seven members a quorum for all ordinary business, because it seems more would not attend their meetings, show that even the trustees were not very careful in regard to their duties. The course of study in Transylvania Seminary was laid out by a committee of the board early in Mr. Toulmin's administration, probably at his suggestion, and arrangements were made to enlarge the library. It is rather interesting to note the curriculum laid down and the scope of the work then done and the ideas of classification then in use.

The following division of subjects is given: professional, the Greek, Latin, and French languages and Bookkeeping; non-professional, Geometry, Geography, Politics, Composition, Elocution, Moral Philosophy, Astronomy, History, Logic and Natural Philosophy.

Additional library facilities were at this time secured by the foundation on Oct. 8th, 1894 of what is now the city library of Lexington, then first established by a stock company on the share plan and for some time located in the Seminary building.

Mr. Toulmin was unanimously re-elected at the end of his first year's service, but voluntarily retired on April 4th, 1796. In a letter in the Kentucky Gazette on April 9th, 1796, he gives as the principal reason for his withdrawal, the smallness of the salary attached to the office, but also intimates that the state of public opinion in regard to the school was not very satisfactory, owing probably to the contest which arose at the time of his first election. Some acts[1] of the legislature passed during his administration, which were calculated to interfere with the powers and rights of the trustees, but which seem never to have been pressed to any definite result, are probably evidences of this dissatisfaction. The financial condition of the school had improved somewhat as it was arranged on June 10th, 1795 to erect a dormitory for it at a cost of $1073, derived from the rent of the Seminary lands. Soon after his retirement from the Seminary, Mr. Toulmin became Secretary of State under Gov. Garrard and was subsequently a Federal judge in Alabama.

On Sept. 23rd, 1796, Rev. James Moore was again called to the head of the Seminary, with the same salary as that of his predecessor.

(1) One, passed Nov. 21, 1795, suspended the trustees from office until the end of that legislative session and another, passed Dec. 21st, 1795 put them under the control of the Court in the Judicial District in which they met.

The active rivalry between it and Kentucky Academy seems to have ceased as soon as Mr. Toulmin, whose election had caused the separation, had resigned. The members of the two boards most deeply interested in the cause of education, particularly Judge Wallce, seem soon to have thought of the union of the two schools, desiring to build up an institution that might be a credit and honor to the state, by combining the two endowments. Moderation and good sense prevailing, this commendable object was at length accomplished after considerable discussion and deliberation. A proposition for the union came from the Academy trustees as early as June 3rd, 1796, and on Sept. 23rd of that year was reported on by a committee of the Seminary trustees as "for the public good" and "consistent with the laws." (1) On Oct. 10th, following, committees of the two boards agreed upon a plan of union practically the same as that subsequently adopted, but for some reason, although it was at first accepted by the Seminary board the next day, this was debated and discussed at intervals for over two years, whether on account of the Academy trustees insisting, as one of the conditions of union, that the students should be required to attend prayers daily and church service on Sunday does not appear, although this was in the terms proposed by the Academy trustees and may have been one of the questions at issue.

Meanwhile Transylvania Seminary, although apparently growing more prosperous, as is shown by the appointment, on Oct. 10th, 1797, at the same time that Mr. Moore was unanimously re-elected, of a French teacher at a salary of $50 and the tuition in his department, even made propositions for union to another school in Lexington, Lexington Academy; but finally, on Nov. 2nd, 1798, the union with Kentucky Academy was definitely

(1) Records of the Board of Trustees of Transylvania Seminary.

agreed upon. This union was upon joint petition of the two boards, drawn up on Nov. 3rd, 1798, consummated by an act of the State Legislature, on Dec. 22nd, 1798.(1) This action was not endorsed by "Father" Rice and some other promoters and friends of Kentucky Academy, who still mistrusted the management of Transylvania Seminary, but was largely brought about by the influence of Judge Wallace, a friend of both schools and of the cause of education in general. It was, as we have seen, only part of a splendid educational plan of which the academy act of the same date was another part, for the conception of which, Judge Wallace is entitled to imperishable honor.

-The University proper-

Jan. 1st, 1799, the day on which the act of Dec. 22nd, 1798 went into effect, may be truly called the natal day of Transylvania University, as the combined institution was called in the act of union. The history of the University from this time forward may be, in general, according to Collins, divided into four periods as follows:
Frist,- That from 1799 to 1818; second,- that from 1818 to 1827; third,- from 1827 to 1849 and fourth,- from 1849 to 1865.

-Period from 1799 to 1818-

The joint petition of the two boards to the legislature asking for the act of union is of interest as showing the ideas and purposes had in view in their action. The main cause of its preamble reads as follows: "That the respective boards of the said trustees contemplating the many singular advantages to be derived to this remote country from therein a University, well endowed and properly conducted; more especially as by this measure only, many of our youths can be prevented from going into other countries to complete their education, where they must greatly

---

(1) Toulmin's Acts of Ky., pp. 467-469; Littell's Laws of Ky., vol II, pp. 234-236.

Then follows the plan of union which will not be quoted at length. It was simply in effect an enlargement of the Transylvania Seminary act of 1783, as the laws regulating the Seminary were to be those regulating the University, unless altered by the legislature *upon* joint petition of a majority of its new board of trustees, and the seat of the University was to be Lexington, unless changed by a two-thirds vote of that board. The more distinctive outlines of a University are to be seen in the new charter in the extension somewhat of the already ample powers conferred by the Seminary charter, in the arrangement of a broad plan of possible union with other schools, in the system of preparatory schools provided for, as noticed in connection with the history of the early University system, and in the establishment of free scholarships for deserving poor students.

The new institution, by the union of the funds of the Academy and Seminary, also began to have quite a respectable endowment for the time. Kentucky Academy, according to a report of a committee of its trustees made O. 11th, 1796[2], possessed nearly $8000 in cash, reliable subscriptions, books and apparatus, besides the six thousand acres of land later given to it by the state; while Transylvania Seminary had, besides its ed-

(1) Records of the Board of Trustees of Transylvania Seminary.
(2) £ 2298 s. 14 d. 10 3/4, Records of Trustees of Transylvania Seminary.

ucational plant in Lexington, fourteen thousand acres of land, having as Davidson (1) tells us secured an additional six thousand acres under the general academy act of 1798, thus making the combined land endowment according to various estimates, to be worth from $40,000 to $179,000. He also informs us that the combined chemical and philosophical apparatus of the new institution was good, and that its library numbered 1300 volumes.

The legislature had selected, as trustees, the list of twenty-one names submitted to them in the petition, instead of accepting the other alternative proposed, to unite the two old boards and not allow any vacancies to be filled, until twenty-one members were left. The new board was made up of eight members selected from each of the old ones, and five others, including Judge Wallace, John Bradford, George Nicholas, James Garrard, and other prominent public men, and was constituted in such a manner as to give the Presbyterians a representation of one half or more of the whole. The new body was on the same co-optative basis as the old one, and unfortunately some of the old factional spirit seems to have remained among its members. Rev. James Moore, now an Episcopalian, was continued at the head of the new University as its President and had associated with him in its faculty, Rev. James Blythe, M. D., D. D. and Rev. Robert Stuart, both Presbyterians, the respective chairs of the three being Mental Philosophy, Logic and Belles-Lettres, Mathematics and Natural Philosophy, and Languages.

The President's salary was $500 and certain perquisites, including a residence while that of the professors was $400 each. At their first meeting under the new regime, on Jan. 8th, 1799, the trustees gave the institution the appearance of a real University by appointing Hon. George Nich

olas, professor of Law and Politics and Drs. Samuel Brown and Frederick Ridgely, professors respectively of chemistry and Surgery (I).

Mr. Nicholas had been prominent in Virginia, especially in the convention that adopted the Federal constitution, and is called by Butler (2) practically author of the first constitution of Kentuckey, to which state he had come shortly before the meeting of its first constitutional convention, and "the most eminent lawyer of his time, whether his learning or his powers of mind be regarded". He began a course of instruction in law in the University to a class of about nineteen students, among whom it appears were William T. Barry and others, subsequently celebrated in Kentuckey history, but died before the end of the year, the further lectures and the examination of his class being taken charge of on August 7th of that year by a committee of the trustees, themselves prominent lawyers.

Dr. Brown is famous being the first (3) regular medical professor in the West, and for his achievements in the introduction of vaccination into America. He was connected with the medical faculty of the University until 1806 and again from 1819 to 1828.

(1) The transcript of the minutes of the trustees examined by the writer call these chairs, simply chairs of Medicine. They are given in the text as usually stated in most authorities. Peter's Transylvania University, p. 77, gives them as Chemistry, Anatomy and Surgery, amd Materia Medica, Midfery and Practice of Physic. It is quite certain that Dr. Ridgely gave the lectures he delivered soon after this on surgery.

(2) History of Kentuckey, p. 206

(3) He was appointed before Dr. Ridgely, Dr. Brown vaccinated as many as 500 people in Lexington and vicinity before any other physician in America would try the experiment.

Dr. Ridgely is noted as being the first to deliver medical lectures in the West and as being the preceptor of the celebrated Dr. B. W. Dudley, afterwards so long and successfully connected with the University faculty. Dr. Ridgely lectured about this time to a class of six medical students, but seems to have done so in an individual capacity, as both his appointment and that of Dr. Brown, as professors in the University, seem to have been, at this early period, merely nominal.

On October 18th 1799, Hon. James Brown, a member of a family then and since very prominent in the history of the state, became Mr. Nicholas' successor as Professor of Law. This chair for the remainder of this period was occupied for short intervals by Henry Clay, who was elected Oct. 10th, 1805, James Monroe, elected Oct. 16th, 1807, John Pope, elected March first 1814, and John Breckinridge, elected April 18th, 1817, all of whom probably lectured more or less.

On Nov. 4th, 1799, Rev. James Welch succeeded Rev. Robert Stuart as professor of Languages. He held the position until July 17th, 1801, when some difficulty with the students caused him to resign and, on July 23rd following, Alexander McKeehan was elected to the chair. Considerable trouble seems, for some reason, to have been connected with this chair, for we find that, on Oct. 7th, 1802, Rev. Andrew Steele, formerly connected with Kentucky Academy, succeeded Mr. McKeehan, and that on Nov. 3rd, 1803, he was succeeded by James Hamilton and he in turn, on Oct. 1st, 1804, by Ebenezer Sharpe, who was either more fortunate or more efficient than his predecessors for he held the position until the end of this period.

    We know that the number of students in attendance upon the University was not large about the end of this period and there were probably comparatively few (1) during Mr. Moore's presidency.

(1) Davidson tells us that at the close of the century, there were 45 students in the academic department, 19 law students and 6 medical students. For further statements in regard to the early attendance, see Peter's

A college course of fairly good compass for the time was however, maintained and, on April 7th, 1802, the first degree granted by the institution, that of A. B., was conferred on Robert R. Barr. On Oct. 6th of the same year, the same degree was conferred on Josiah Stoddard Johnston and Augustine C. Respass. Mr. Johnston subsequently became United States Senator from Louisiana.

For some reason, not apparent, a misunderstanding seems soon to have arisen between Mr. Moore and the trustees, and, on Oct. 4th, 1804, Dr. Blythe was asked to act as President, while still retaining his professorship and, on Nov. 4th, following, Mr. Moore having resigned the presidency, his chair was filled by the appointment of Rev. Robert H. Bishop,A who held the position until 1824. (1) Mr. Moore did not, however, lose his interest in the institution or sever his connection with it entirely, as we find he became a trustee in 1805 and remained one for sometime afterwards. He subsequently devoted himself mainly to the work of his church, becoming, in 1809, the first regular rector of Christ's Episcopal Church in Lexington. He was distinguished for his learning, piety, and courtesy and had done considerable under the circumstances toward laying the foundation of Transylvania's future prosperity. (2)

Rev. Dr. Blythe remained as acting President of the University until near the end of this period, during which time the institution grew in a sound and healthy though moderate way. The course of instruction in its academic department was soon brought up to an equality with that of the Eastern colleges, except in the classics which were then regarded as of somewhat secondary importance, in the West, and, on Oct. 31st, 1812, an

(1) He resigned at that time to become President of Miami University, Ohio
(2) A short sketch of Dr. Moore is to be found in Collin's History of Ky., vol I, p. 442.

extra teacher was added to the faculty of this department in the person of John B. Fouchier who was made instructor in French.

Dr. Blythe also endeavored to develop the professional departments, especially that of medicine. Dr. Elisha Warfield had already in 1802 been added to the medical faculty, as yet only prospective, as professor of Surgery and Midwifery, and, in 1805, Rev. James Fishback, M. D., was appointed to the chair of Theory and Practice of Medicine, thus making with Dr. Brown, who held the chair of Chemistry, what may be called the first regular faculty of the department. No teaching was however done at this time and all the professors resigned their chairs in 1806. On April 8th, 1809, a more complete faculty was organized, among whom the celebrated Dr. Dudley appears for the first time. The professors and their chairs were as follows: Dr. B. W. Dudley, Anatomy and Physiology; Dr. Joseph Buchanan, Institutes of Medicine; Dr. James Overton, Materia Medica and Dr. Elisha Warfield, Surgery and Midwifery. Dr. Dudley remained in this faculty one or two years but neither he nor any of his colleagues seem to have delivered any lectures at this time.

Another organization (1) of the faculty took place on Nov. 11th, 1815 when Drs. Thomas Cooper, B. W. Dudley, Coleman Rogers, Samuel Brown, William H. Richardson and Charles W. Short were elected to chairs. All of these, however, declined except Drs. Dudley and Richardson, the former of whom lectured regularly in his department of Surgery and the latter, a small amount, in 1816-17, a committee of the trustees reporting to this effect on Feb. 22nd, 1817, when it is also stated that Dr. Richardson had fifteen or sixteen students in his department of Midwifery and would lecture regularly in the future. On Dec. 10th, 1816, Dr. Daniel Drake

(1) The first names of Drs. Cooper and Rogers are here taken from Peter's Transylvania University, pp. 95-96 where the chairs of all these prospective professors are also given.

was elected professor of Materia Medica and, o. Feb. 2..., 1817, Dr. James Overton became professor of Theory and Practice of Medicine and Dr. Blythe was transferred to the chair of Chemistry. These, with Drs. Dudley and Richardson, became the first active medical faculty of Transylvania University. They lectured regularly during the session of 1817-18 to a class of about twenty students and, in 1818, the first medical commencement in the Mississippi Valley was held at Lexington, the degree of M. D. being conferred on one candidate, John L. McCullough.

The funds of the institution also improved during this period. The greater part of the original endowment grant of 8000 acres of land, which had been previously leased for long terms at a low rate, had been sold about 1812 for $30000 which was invested in stock of the Bank of Kentuckey and with its increments and the income accruing from other sources, Davidson (1) tells us, made the money endowment of the institution in 1812, $67532.
We now begin to find many resolutions passed by the trustees looking
toward the erection of a new building, the means for which were to be at least partly obtained by selling a portion of the old Campus which was to be divided by having streets run through it. (2) Steps were also taken with a view of securing "a gentleman of ability and talents" for president.

(1) Presbytarian Church in Ky. p. 297., Davidson says the sale of lands occured about 1806 but the records of the trustees show that the principal sale occured in 1812.
(2) Mill and market streets were run through it at this period and a small strip on the west, cut off by Mill street, sold to Thomas January for $1-000. The running through of a street from east to west and the sale of one half of the campus thus divided, was also discussed.

John C. Pope an (I)and finally Rev.Horace Holley,was
fully invited by the trustees to accept the presidency of the University and then this action was rescinded i favor of retaining
Dr.Blythe.There were evidently factions (2) in the board,and strong
differences of opinion as to the proper policy to be pursued,rumors
of which soon began to reach the public ear,for,as early as Dec.30
th.,1815,we hear of a legislative committee being appointed to inquire into the state of the institution in answer to which action
the board issued an address to the public and on Feb.3rd,1816 appointed a committee to defend the University before the State Senate
against caluminating reports,and two days later John Pope was employed as counsel for that purpose.

In 1816 the University grounds were ornamented with shrubbery and
otherwise greatly improved and also considerably enlarged through
the liberality of several friends of the institution,including the
celebrated statesman Henry Clay.The Higgins Lot,nowth western part
of the Ken. cky University campus,having been acquired in the latter part of this year partly by donation and partly by purchase.In
1817 the erection of a large and handsome new building was begun.It
was completed in 1818,was located near the center of the old campus,
was three stories in height and contained their rooms.It included

a prominent Baptist clergyman had been called to the presidency in March, 1816 and in April 1817, Philip Linsey, later so long the distinguished president of the University of Nashville, was elected to the position. These both declined and on Oct. 25th, 1817, Dr. Holley was again balloted for, ineffectually at that time, but on November 25th following, he was unanimously elected at a salary of $2250 (1) per annum, an amount which shows the improved financial condition of the University. After a visit to Lexington, during the following summer, Dr. Holley formally accepted the position.

Dr. Blythe had, on March 23rd, 1816, after one or two previous resignations which he had been induced to withdraw, finally resigned his professorship and with it, the acting presidency of the University. He had remained at its head for twelve years during which time it had made considerable progress. He was too exclusive to be popular but was a diligent and efficient teacher and a man of ability. Collins (2) tells us that he had "native strength of character, prompt decision and a practical turn which enabled him to acquit himself well in every situation." On Feb. 28th, 1817, he was elected professor of Chemistry in the medical department of the University which was then first regularly opened, a position which he retained until 1831. Just prior to his resignation in 1816, the trustees had furnished him with $1000 for the purchase of apparatus for the chemical department.

On Feb. 3rd, 1818 occurred what may be called the closing incident of this period of the University's history. On that date, at whose so-

licitation it does not appear, an act (1) was passed by the legislature removing the old board of trustees and appointing a new one of thirteen members, eight of them being at the time members of the old board and another, Henry Clay, having been formerly so. The new body was composed of prominent public men of excellent merit but of no special religious pretensions or connections. The religious apprehensions of the Presbyterians, especially of the old board, already perhaps considerably aroused by the alleged Socinianism (2) of Dr. Holley, the new President, whose last election had been unanimous because they had refused to take any part in it, were further intensified by this action which they considered dangerous in its religious tendencies and which they also regarded as illegal (3), in that it had not been petitioned for by a majority of the trustees, as required by the charter. We shall find these

(1) Acts of 1818, pp. 554-556-- among the thirteen trustees were Henry Clay, Robert Trimble, Edmund Bullock, John T. Mason Jr., Robert Wickliffe, Joh Pope, John Brown and Charles Humphreys.

(2) This had been noised abroad somewhat at the time of his first election on Nov. 11th, 1815 and was probably the cause of that action being rescinded later when a committee was appointed to inquire into Dr. Holly's character.

(3) The language of the charter and the position taken by previous legislatures certainly gave them good grounds for taking this position. The act of 1783 had merely declared that the said trustees shall at all times be accountable for their transactions touching any matter or anything relating to said Seminary in such manner as the legislature shall direct." The natural inference from this was that they might be removed from office, or otherwise punished for malfeasance but not that their organization could be altered except according to the provisions of the charter itself. This was the construction put upon that charter by the acts of Nov. 21st, 1795 and Dec. 21st, 1795 which did not reorganize the old board but merely suspended them from office in the one case and in the other, made them accountable for the discharge of their duties to the District Court. The position taken by the Presbyterians was at least as tenable as the opposite one given in Peter's Transylvania University, pp. 22-24.

circumstances rather adverse to the interests of the University in raising up against it a strong religious prejudice in the public mind generally and in causing the Presbyterians particularly to be very unfavorably disposed toward the new administration and very much inclined to withdraw their patronage, as we shall soon see them doing. At the same time, this act of reorganization had its beneficial effect as expressed by a committee of the two houses of the legislature in 1827, in taking Transylvania University "into their more immediate protection" (2) and attempting to make of it more distinctively a state institution and to build it up into a great University under state auspices. The old board, in view of their going out of office issued on Feb. 26th, 1818, an address on the interests and prospects of the University, the former of which they considered of great public importance, the latter very flattering. This was their last official act.

The attendance during this early part of the institution's history was not large as the records of the trustees report, on Oct. 18th, 1817, that there had been seventy-seven students the past session (2). The slow growth in the number of students may be partly accounted for by the preoccupation of the people in other matters and by the constant elevation of the standard of scholarship which made entrance more difficult. Hon. Robert Wickliffe the President of the new board of trustees of 1818 says in a notice in Niles' Register (3) that the College is to give an education "as good as is given in other colleges in the United States." There had been altogether, including honorary degrees, only twenty-two de-

(1) Davidson's Presbyterian Church in Ky., p. 315.

(2) Niles' Register, vol. XXIII, p. 387, tells us there were 60 students in the academical department in the summer of 1818.

(3) vol. XV., p. 132.

- Period from 1818 to 1827 -

Dr. Holley's (1) administration, extending fro November 1818 to March 1827, is by far the most brilliant era of the University's history. The new President aimed to make of Transylvania a genuine University, complete in every college and liberally endowed. He was in many ways admirably fitted for the undertaking. Having graduated at Yale, in the class of 1803, when about twenty-two years of age, he had after studying law for a while in New York and then abandoning it for the ministry, pursued the study of theology under Dr. Dwight in New Haven where he had become a Unitarian, not from his preceptor but from personal conviction. Since 1809, he had been the pastor of the Hollis Street Unitarian Church of Boston, Mass., here he was greatly beloved and admired. He was a man of engaging manners and of great personal magnetism. Besides, his learning was very wide and his eloquence so stirring as to cause a staid New England audience to burst into noisy applause on the occasion of his delivering a sermon before the Ancient and Honorable Artillery Company of Boston. In Lexington, he entertained freely patrons of learning and distinguished strangers and captivating, as he did, all who came near him, was calculated to interest them in the welfare of the University. This he did in a very successful way in the case of the state legislature and of such public spirited citizens as Col. James Morrison, Henry Clay and others.

The circumstances were also favorable for a new era of progress as the state had just emerged, with great credit to herself, from the war of

(1) For more extended sketches of Dr. Holley, see Collin's History of Ky. vol. II., pp. 217-218 and especially Dr. Charles Caldwell's Discourse on the Genius and Character of Rev. Horace Holley.

timely.

Dr. Holley was formally inaugurated on Dec. 19th, 1818 and at once set to work to build up the institution, and proving, in many ways, the man for the place, the University entered upon a career of almost marvelous prosperity, in which the plans of Judge Wallace seemed about to be realized. The faculty was soon reorganized and enlarged and men of reputation called to the various chairs largely through the President's personal influence. Its personnel in October 1821 was as follows:

-Academical Department-

Rev. Horace Holley, A. M., LL. D., President --- Philology, Belles Lettres and Mental Philosophy.

Rev. R. H. Bishop, A. M.,   Natural Philosophy and History.

J. F. Jenkins, A. B.,   Mathematics.

John Roche, A. M.   Languages.

Constantine S. Rofinesque,   Natural History, Botany and Modern Languages.

J. W. Tibbats and B. O. Peers,-   Tutors.

-Medical College-

James Blythe, M. D., D. D.   Chemistry.

                              -Law School-

William S. Barry,   Professor.

    Dr. Daniel Drake was soon added to the medical faculty and Judge Jesse Bledsoe to the law faculty.

    Prof. C. S. Rafinesque (1) who held the chair of Natural Science in the Academical department and of medical botany in the medical department was connected with the University from 1819 to 1825 and was probably at the time, the most eminent scientist in America.

    In 1824, he established in connection with the University, a Botanical Garden which, however, was not a financial success, and was not long kept up. He is the author of a number of scientific works and although somewhat visionary, did much valuable teaching.

    The professional departments especially were developed by Dr. Holley, and the medical college, which had been again suspended in 1818, but was revived in 1819, soon began to hold a prominent rank not only in the West but in the country at large. Its library, secured by a special visit of Dr. Caldwell to the Continent in 1820, was so rare and valuable, many of the books being those of eminent French physicians ruined by the Revolution, as to make it superior to anything of its kind in America. The number of students in this department grew from twenty students and one graduate in 1817-18 to 281 students and 53 graduates in 1825-26, there being 93 students in 1820-21, 138 in 1821-22, 170 in 1822-23, 200 in 1823-24 and 234 in 1824-25. (2) Its faculty was also unexcelled in the country for their talents and acquirements. We have already noticed Dr. Brown's

1799 to 1806.

Dr. Caldwell (1) had been formerly a member of the faculty of the University of Pennsylvania and was very noted both as a physician and teacher. He was connected with the Transylvania medical faculty from 1819 to 1837.

Dr. Drake (2) long one of the most eminent medical professors in the West, in the medical College of Cincinnati and Louisville as well as Lexington, was connected with the Transylvania University faculty from 1823 to 1826 as well as in 1817-18.

Dr. F. W. Dudley,(3) long the most eminent surgeon in the Mississippi Valley, if not in the whole country, famed especially for his operations in Lithotomy and upon the eye and cranium as well as other delicate operations, was a great teacher as well. An alumnus of Transylvania University and a graduate of the University of Pennsylvania in Medicine, he had pursued the study of his chosen profession for four years in London and Paris. He entered the Transylvania medical faculty regularly in 1817 and remained in it constantly for forty years, contributing in no small measure to its great success by his personal efforts and reputation. Drs. Richardson and Blythe were also noted as successful teachers in their respective departments.

Dr. Drake tells us in speaking of this faculty and of the law faculty at this time, "that they were men of brilliant talents and wide reputation and collectively constituted a greater array of strength and bril-

(1) For further sketch see Collin's History of Ky., vol. II., p. 219; Collin's Sketches of Ky., pp. 558-559.

liacy than was scarcely ever collected in any institute at one time."(1)
Much valuable research and investigation was carried on at the University
at this time by its medical faculty, the results of which were made known
through the Transylvania Medical Journal which they then published.
This faculty was further strengthened, either during this period or soon
after, by the addition of such eminent professors as Drs. John Esten Cooke
L. P. Yandell, H. H. Eaton and Charles W. Short, most of whom remained
connected with it for many years afterwards. For sometime to come with
its distinguished corps of professors, its excellent chemical and anatomical apparatus and its unsurpassed library, it may fairly be claimed to
have been the equal of any medical school in the country in equipment
and was only excelled in numbers by the medical department of the University of Pennsylvania.

President Holley not only thus enlarged and strengthened the professional departments, but, as a means toward this end and toward the
general building up of the University, was able to induce the legislature, and Lexington(2) to contribute to the wants of the institution more
liberally than ever before. In 181-, the legislature granted to the
University, the bonus of the Farmers and Mechanics' Bank for two years,
amounting to $3000; in 1820, $5000 from the state treasury to buy books
and apparatus for the medical college; in 1821, one half the net profits
of the Lexington branch of the Bank of the Commonwealth for two years,

(1) Mansfield's Memoirs, p. 128.

(2) For these various appropriations, see Report of the Superintendent
of Public Instruction of Ky. for 1875-76, pp. 15-16 appendix; Autobiography of Dr. Charles Caldwell, p. 360; also Acts of 1818-19, pp. 692-693;
of 1819-20, p. 952 and of 1822-23, pp. 149-151 and 160-162.

yielding $20,00, which was, however, only equivalent to $10000 in specie; in 1822, a lottery privilege of $25000 for a new medical building, and also 2% of the auction sales in Fayette County for a law library; in 1824, $20000 from the state treasury. Lexington, in 1820, also gave $6000 for the equipment of the medical college, and, in 1822, citizens of the town contributed about $5000 (1) more. These would be considered rather small donations now-a-days to a state educational enterprise, but were the quite liberal for the time and circumstances. They were however always given against strong opposition in the legislature and were companied by other legislation in some respects adverse to the University.(2) We shall soon find that when the old opposition becomes strengthened by popular dissatisfaction in regard to the administration of the University, all state appropriations are entirely withdrawn.

Unfortunately, all the early donations instead of being added to the endowment of the institution, had to be used to pay its debts and supply it with books and apparatus. The result was that, in 1825, few colleges in the country had better libraries and internal equipment generally than Transylvania University, but there were little means for the institution's future expansion. The attention of benevolently minded individuals was, however, being attracted to the University by its work under Dr. Holley as is shown by the bequest of Col. James Morrison (3) who had been for some time the chairman of its board of trustees and who died on April 23rd

Circumstances, as we have seen, were favorable and as Dr. Holley's objectionable opinions and actions were not generally known for sometime, he was able by his great executive ability to build up the institution very rapidly, and to make its name known, not only in the state but throughout the country, and even in Europe. The Governors of the stat soon began, in their messages, to speak of the honor and lustre it reflected upon Kentucky and its graduates soon began to be important factors in the life of the South and West from which sections most of them came. The relative importance of the University among American colleges during the early part of this period may be shown somewhat by the fact that in March 1821 (2), it had 282 students while Yale had 319, Harvard 286, Union 264, Dartmouth, 222 and Princeton, 150. Of the Transylvania students, 185 were at that time in the Academical department.(3)

But Dr. Holley's religious opinions, supposed by many to verge on infidelity, soon began to be noised abroad, as also his love of worldly amustment, equally objectionable to many, and, by reason of the prejudice

(1) Or library by the will, but the trustees chose the professorship.

(2) Statistics from Niles' Register vol. XXIX., p. 3, vol. XXXI., p. 158 of this work gives the total number of graduates of other colleges i 1826 as follows: Harvard, 53; Yale, 100; Princeton, 24; Amherst, 32; Dartmouth, 37 and Union 71. The following degrees conferred by Transylvania (taken mainly from the American Journal of Education for 1826, pp. 311-313) will serve for a comparison later in this period: in 1823, 32 A.B.'s (B.L.'s and M.D.'s not given); in 1824, 24 A.B.'s, 16 B.L.'s and 47 M.D.'s in 1825, 32 A.B.'s, 16 B.L.'s and 57 M.D.'s.

and sectarian animosity of the day, soon began to cause criticism
and opposition. The Presbyterians had early become alarmed and
soon after his election had again determined to have an institution
undoubtedly under their control- a movement resulting in the founding
of Centre College in 1819. The Catholics founded St. Joseph's
in the same year and St. Mary's in 1821, and the Methodists Augusta,
in 1822. The same denominational idea was prominent in the establishment
of Cumberland College by the Cumberland Presbyterians in
1827, and later, of Georgetown College by the Baptists in 1829 and
of Bacon College by the Christians in 1836.

Opposition on the part of the general public, through the Press
and otherwise, also soon began to manifest itself and, as early as
1824, Professors Barry, Bledsoe, and others, connected with the
faculty of the University, deemed it wise to issue a pamphlet defending
Dr. Holley against unjust calumnies. The former opposition
of the legislature also increased in response to the state of public
opinion, as was perhaps first shown by the reorganization of the
board of trustees in 1821 (1), when four new members were added to
its number. Committees of investigation into the condition of the
University, which was accused of extravagance, began to be frequently
appointed soon after this and hindrance rather than help was to be
expected in the future from the state.

Discouraged and irritated by the state of public opinion, and
harassed by charges which he felt to be unmerited, Dr. Holley, despairing,
as he did, of the further enlargement of the University,
especially through state aid, felt constrained to resign, offering

his resignation at first to take effect in Jan. 1827. He withdrew
this resignation at the solicitation of friends but on Jan. 18th,
1827, finally resigned, to take effect in the following March, greatly to the regret of the majority of the citizens of Lexington, of
the trustees and of the students, a number of the latter leaving the
institution upon his retirement. He left Lexington on March 27th,
1827 to engage in other educational enterprises in Louisiana and
died of yellow fever on July 31st following, while on his way by
sea to New York.

He certainly had done much for the University, as shown by its
remarkable growth during his administration. He is however not
entitled to all the credit for the most brilliant period of institution's history for, as we have seen, he was greatly aided by
favorable circumstances which, under any fairly good management,
would have caused a considerable expansion in the University's sphere.
A great deal of the foundation of its prosperity had been laid under
the conservative, but careful, administration of Dr. Blythe.
The academical department had been brought up to the proportions of
a college, the law department inaugurated and the medical department
somewhat fairly started out. A great deal of the success of this
last department is to be attributed to the energy and ability of Dr.
Dudley who had already become fully identified with the department
in 1815 and had become a member of its first regular faculty in 1817.
Dr. Drake tells us that the prosperity of the medical school was
mainly due " to the public spirit and the exertions of Dr. Dudley."(1
Before the advent of the Holley era, the institution had already acquired considerable local reputation and was beginning to attract the

(1) Mansfield's Memoirs, p. 120.

favorable attention of the state authorities, not much through the
personal influence and efforts of Dr. Blythe we know not.
Gov. Slaughter, in his message of Dec. 2 d, 1817, recommended that
Transylvania University, which he says "will soon hold an eminent
rank among the institutions of learning in the United States," be
extended such aid as will place it "on the most respectable footing."

Dr. Holley is however entitled to much praise and credit for
the institution's success on account of his power of increasing the
interest in it of public men like Henry Clay and benevolently minded
men like Col. Morrison, by reason of his influence with the state
authorities, as is evidenced by the favorable tone of the Governor's
messages during the greater part of his administration, and the legislative appropriations secured during that period and also for his
energy and great executive ability, as well as his advanced ideas
on education. The recommendations contained in his last report to
the trustees are quite modern in tone and are in some respects certainly quite in advance of the ideas then prevalent. He recommends(1)
the creation of a regular professorship of Modern Languages, the increase of the law professorships to four, one of which should treat
exclusively of Roman law, the establishment of a gymnasium, the col-
lection of a cabinet of minerals, the foundation of a gallery of
Fine Arts, and a regular arrangement for the establishment of libraries in the different departments, especially that of History and
Politics. The works to be added to the library were to be largely
for the use of advanced students, and of the professors, and special
attention was to be given to the course of Economic Science.

Some idea of the growth of the University during this period may
be obtained from the increase in size of its general library and the

addition to its roll of Alumni. The former, as seen by Dr. Holley's last report (1), had increased from about 1300 volumes to about 5500 volumes and the number of degrees conferred were now 666 instead of 22 as previously, 40 of these were honorary, but the remainder had been obtained by completing a course the standard of which had been constantly elevated. There had been, up to this time, 327 graduates in the medical department and 41 in the law department.

Dr. Holley was undoubtedly much esteemed by most of those who came in the closest personal contact with him. With all the admirable qualifications for the position he filled, which we have seen him to possess and with the high rank and recognition he had been able to secure for the University, it seems a great pity that he should not have been able to so conduct himself, and that too honorably, as to avoid precipitating a conflict with prejudice and animosities which however unreasonable they may have appeared to him, he might have known his opposing could not change but would only provoke counter irritation and resistance. He was undoubtedly much misjudged and maligned, but it is also true that his own indiscreet words and conduct were responsible to a considerable extent for these actions. Although his motives should not be questioned, yet hardly so much can be said for his judgement.

- Period from 1827 to 1849 -

We now enter the third period of the University's history which will witness the adoption by the trustees of a new plan of supporting and building up the institution. Under the act of 1818 and again, by that of 1821, which in effect only changed their number, the trustees were to be appointed by the legislature every two years but by

(1) Caldwell's Memoirs, p. 193

the neglect of this provision, it seems that the had been allowed
to become, as formerly, practically a self-perpetuating body, who
were free to manage the institution according to their own ideas
which, during this period, were not materially at least, interfered with by the legislature. As we have seen by reason of the
adverse condition of public opinion, the University had been virtual-
ly abandoned by the state, and was to receive no more state help for
nearly thirty years. Without this assistance upon which it had so
long depended, as its own resources were insufficient, it would naturally have had to struggle on in rather a poor way in the future.
The trustees therefore sought to bring to it the needed help through
partial denominational control, or at least the use of denominational influence and patronage. The institution was placed first under
Baptist, then Episcopal, again Presbyterian, and lastly Methodist
auspices, prominent ministers of these denominations being successively called to its presidency in the hope that thereby the support
of their church organization might be secured for it.

The control exercised by these denominations was in each case
only partial and their patronage, in itself, always insufficient,
so, in order for it to be at all efficacious, there had to be some outside assistance, and as the state would not furnish this, it came from
local sources, from the friends of the University in Lexington and
from the town itself. We find, soon after the resignation of Dr.
Holley, a number of its local friends rallying around the institution and subscribing for its maintenance a conditional emergency
fund of $3000 a year, for four years, of which amount about $11,000
seems to have been finally paid in. With this help and the pro-
ceeds of the lottery of 1825 and perhaps something from an earlier

one of 1804 (1), instituted for the same purpose, the returns from both of which are quite uncertain in amount, new and spacious medical hall was projected, the corner-stone of which was laid with imposing ceremonies on April 26th 1827. This building which was handsome and well equipped, was completed soon afterwards. It was located where the present city library of Lexington now stands. Prior to its completion, the medical lectures were doubtless given in the main college building.

The resignation of Dr. Holley was of course, under the circumstances, a considerable shock to the University. There was an immediate loss of a number of students, and the attendance the next session was naturally considerably decreased, especially in the academic department. Even in the medical department, which was now quite well established and was less directly affected by the change of administration, the number of students fell off from 241 to 190 the next year.

The academic faculty (2) after Dr. Holley's departure, was composed as follows: John Roche, Professor of Greek and Latin; Rev. George T. Chapman, Professor of History and Antiquity; Rev. B. O. Peers, Professor of Moral Philosophy; and Thomas J. Matthews, Professor of Mathematics. No new president was at once elected, but it was arranged that the academic department should be managed by its faculty and that Drs. Caldwell, Dudley and Short, of the medical faculty, should preside in succession on all public occasions.

During the future history of the University the professional
department somewhat overshadows its other parts. They were conducted upon a somewhat independent basis and being largely self-supporting by reason of their reputation and their celebrated faculties,
especially with the aid of the local financial help which was mainly
bestowed upon them, they were in the main prosperous and were not
greatly affected by the ups and downs of the literary department.
After Dr. Holley had left, they maintained themselves fairly well
for the immediate future and there was no reason why the University
as a whole should not have continued to succeed, if it had not been
abandoned by the state, and indeed, for the time, to a considerable
extent, by every one, some public spirited citizens of Lexington
excepted. This now becomes a characteristic feature of its history,
especially of its academical department. As it was not sufficiently
endowed to be self-supporting, outside assistance or strong local
support was imperative and when, for any reason, either or both of
these were lacking, it lapsed into a condition of activity, or torpor,
until it was in some way temporarily revived by a new impetus.
This applies especially to the whole period after Dr. Holley's resignation, when regular legislative patronage was withdrawn, but the
decline did not show itself for sometime after that event.

The first denominational experiment of this period was inaugurated in June 1828, by the election of Rev. Alva Woods, D.D., of
Rhode Island, to the vacant presidency of the University. The reputation of the institution was still considerable in the East, as is
shown by the fact that Dr. Woods resigned the presidency of Brown
University to accept its presidential chair. He was a Baptist

been a practical, matter-of-fact man who made very good use of the facilities he had at his command and managed to keep the University in a fair state of prosperity (1) during his administration, which lasted about two years.

His practical energy was well shown in connection with the loss of the main building of the University by fire when temporary quarters were at once secured and not a single day's exercises were suspended nor a single student left the institution. This great misfortune happened on the light of May 9th, 1829 and besides the excellent University building completed in 1818, destroyed the law and societies' libraries and most of the philosophical apparatus. It entailed a loss of about $30,000, exclusive of the insurance, thus practically wiping out all of the original endowment coming from Transylvania Seminary. It, of course, greatly crippled the University's future usefulness and the discouragement due to it was probably the cause of Dr. Woods' resignation, in 1830, to accept the presidency of the rising University of Alabama where he considered he had a more promising field of labor.

There was then an interregnum in the presidency of about three years during which two events of some importance occurred. Dr. Blythe, so long connected with the University faculty, resigned his chair of Chemistry in 1831 to accept the presidency of Hanover Col-

---

(1) A catalogue of the medical department of the University for 1828 shows that there were that year 40 graduates in that department who came from the states of Ky., Miss., Ala., Tenn., S. C., Va., La., Mich. and Ohio. Niles tells us (Register, vol. XXXVII., p. 216) that near the opening of the session of 1828-29, there were 150 students in the medical department and 130 in the college and preparatory classes. A catalogue given for 1829-30, 24 law students, 141 academical students, of whom 49 are in the preparatory classes, and 241 medical students who represent 13 states.

the new administration in March 1833.

The other event referred to above, is the erection of the college building provided for from the residuary estate of Col. James Morrison. It was begun during this interregnum and was located on the eastern part of the Higgins lot acquired by the University in 1816. Afterwards, in 1835, the place of Dr. Blythe's former residence, known as the Blythe lot, now the eastern portion of the Kentucky University campus, was purchased by the trustees, from funds also arising from the Morrison bequest, thus completing a beautiful campus near the center of which the Morrison college building was located.

The Baptists had now begun to transfer their patronage to their own distinctive institution, founded at Georgetown in 1829, and so another source of assistance for the University was sought after by its trustees and in 1833 (2), Rev. B. O. Peers (3), a prominent Episcopal clergyman, was called to its presidency. He was a man of high character and advanced views and was one of the many alumni of Transylvania University now rapidly coming forward into future prominence.

(1) He continued as President of Hanover until 1836 when he resigned on account of bad health. His death occurred in 1842.

(2) For other facts in regard to Rev. P. O. Peers' life, see Colli.'s History of Ky. vol. I, pp. 442-443. Mr. Peers, besides writing numerous articles for news-papers and magazines, is the author of a small work entitled, "Christian Education."

(3) Peter's Transylvania University pp. 160-161 gives the dates of President Peers' inauguration and resignation as respectively 1832 and Feb. 1st, 1834 but the appended sketch of Mr. Peers give these dates as 1833-3: which are given by all of a number of other authorities consulted by the writer.

He had graduated in the class of 1824 on remained tutor in his
Alma Mater for a time. He later studied theology at Princeton and
was, for a while, engaged in church work in Alexandria, Va. From
conscientious reflections, he then decided to enter the profession
of teaching and became, in 1827, Professor of Moral Philosophy in
Transylvania.

He was one who devoted himself with great enthusiasm and
earnestness to whatever he undertook and having thought deeply and
observed widely upon educational problems, was soon quite in advance
of his state and even in some respects of the country in his ideas
and theories. We shall find that he is the virtual founder of the
public school system of Kentucky at least in being the first one who
most prominently and successfully agitated the question of its a-
doption.

On June 1, 1829 (1), he founded in Lexington a Mechanics' Institute on the model of those introduced into Scotland by Dr. John
Anderson, some thirty years before, but at the time of its establishment, quite a new enterprise for this country. In connection with
this Institute, an Apprentices' School was soon opened in which sys-
tematic courses of public lectures were delivered, mainly by professors of Transylvania University. We have in these lectures what
appear to be quite perfect types of modern University Extension
courses. They are reported to have been quite successful for a
time, similar ones being, through their example, instituted at
Louisville and other important points in the state, but for some rea-

(1)This date is variously given by different authorities but the
one accepted here is supported in quite an authentic way by the Barnard's American Journal of Education, vol. XVI., p. 353 and is probably correct.

son, are soon ost sight of.

In 1830,[1] after severing his connection with the University faculty, he had established in Lexington, the Eclectic Institute in which an attempt was made to put into practical operation, as in the Rensellaer Institute at Troy, New York, the principles of Pestalozzi and Fellenberg. This school was quite successful for a time, but was too advanced for its surroundings and so did not last long. Mr. Peers had associated with himself in its faculty, i 1832, two model educators, Henry A. Griswold and Dr. Robert Peter. He was still in charge of the school when elected to the presidency of Transylvania Universuty. As noted above, Dr. Peter went with him into the University faculty.

Another of President Peers' advanced ideas, quite advanced for the time[2] and quite practical, if public opinion had been prepared for it, was to convert Transylvania University into a State Normal School which should have its revenues supplemented by ample state appropriations and should be put at the head of a state public school system. This view is clearly expressed in the address delivered at the time of his inauguration as President of the University. Mr. Peers' ideas seem to have been too advanced for his time and perhaps, too, for his executive ability, although an extraordinary amount of the latter would probably have been needed to pull the

(1) There is much variation in regard to this date as in the case of that of the establishment of the Mechanics' Institute but this seems best authenticated. See Barnard's American Journal of Education, vol. XVII. p. 148.

(2) The Normal School idea had at the time been discussed comparatively little even in New England, and the first regular Normal School w s not opened until July 1839. See Gordy's Rise and Growth of the Normal School Idea in the United States, especially pp. 19 and 47.

ature of the institution's management ap-
during this administration in the establish
ts other departments, of a Theological
of the Episcopal Church. The new depart-
omparatively short while after its estab-
r had any really organic connection with
ly an independent institution (2) temporar-

nt Peers' term of office that the build-
uary estate of Col. Morrison and named in
e, was completed. It was quite a commo-
re, costing about $40,000 and is still
tered, as one of the principal buildings of
was dedicated with elaborate ceremonies on
e same time, President Peers was formal-
having taken the oath of office prescribed
ers by the original charter (3), delivered
he prospects of the University and the
titution.
1835, when he had begun to see the futility
erished plans in regard to the institution,

at in Jan. 1834, there were only 63 stu-
partment, whom 31 were in the prepara-
me however the Law department has 52
enal tment 20, the latter from 15 differ-

he resigned its presidency and entered, in the work of his Church
at Louisville, what he considered wider fields of usefulness.
In 1838, he was transferred to other church work in New York City
where he died in 1842, in the midst of a career promising much for
the future.   He was noted for his ardent piety, sound learning and
zealous devotion to the cause of general education.

His associates in the academic faculty of Transylvania University at the opening of his administration in 1833 (1), in addition
to Dr. Peter, who has been already mentioned, were John Lutz D.P.(2),
Professor of Mathematics; E. Roval, Professor of Languages and
Charles E. Bains, Principal of the Preparatory department. In 1835,
Prof. S. Hebard had taken Prof. Lutz's place in the faculty. The
medical faculty in 1833 included Drs. Dudley Caldwell, Cooke, Richardson, Short and Yandell and the 260 medical students of that year
were from 15 different states, mainly in the South and West.

A few months (3) after Mr. Peers' resignation as president of
the University, he was succeeded in that position, by Rev. Thomas W.
Coit, D.D., who had been a member of the Theological faculty then
associated with the institution and was a high church man of some
celebrity.   President Coit retained his office about three years
which was somewhat longer than the usual presidential term during
this period of the University's history.

In January, 1836, an attempt was made to carry out Pres. Peers'

idea and convert, by the aid of legislative action, the University into a State Normal School, the State contributing $5000 a year to its support and receiving in return free tuition for 100 state students but the plan was too advanced for the legislature to then adopt and we shall see, when about twenty years later another legislature did establish such a school, the idea was still ahead of public opinion and the experiment was destined to be a failure.

President Coit seems to have been an excellent man but perhaps less energetic than President Peers and so less able to stem the tide of general decline in the fortunes of the University which had set in stronger than ever and that even affected the professional departments hitherto comparatively vigorous. This depression resulted, in 1837, in an attempt, participated in by Drs. Caldwell, Cooke, Yandell and Short, the majority of the medical faculty and perhaps others which seems, for a time at least, to have been conducted secretly, to move the medical department bodily to Louisville which had developed into the largest and most important business center in the state and was considered by them in many ways a more eligible location than Lexington, for the school. When this plan became generally known, a storm of local indignation was aroused and the professors who favored the change resigned their chairs, as they may perhaps have done in any event, if their views had not been carried out. They were mainly instrumental, soon after, in establishing, at Louisville, on an independent basis, a rival school called the Louisville Medical Institute which subsequently developed into the medical department of the University of Louisville, but which does not seem, for a time at least, if at all, to have materially injured the medical department of Transylvania University.

Indeed, the movement was upon the whole really beneficial to

and needs and help was brought to bear, in 1838-39, from the same source and partly in the same manner, that it had come several times before. The City of Lexington granted $70,000 to the funds of the institution while a company of seventy of her citizens, organized in a corporate capacity under the name of the Transylvania Institute on Feb. 20th, 1839, subscribed $35,000 for the same purpose, transferable scholarships, carrying with them free tuition, being issued to the city and to the subscribers for each $500 contributed. Of the money given by the city, $40,000 was to go to the construction of a new medical college building and apparatus, another $5,000 was for the library of the law department, and the remainder for the endowment of Morrison College. The money raised by the Transylvania Institute also went to Morrison College, part of it being used to erect a new dormitory. After these additions, the property of the College was estimated to be worth about $100,000 and its endowment, including the Morrison fund, about $75,000. (1) The medical faculty which was reorganized on April 29th, 1837 (2), also came to the rescue by subscribing $3,000 to purchase a new lot for the medical building and afterwards paying off a debt of about $15,000 remaining on that structure after its completion. The corner-stone of this building (3) was laid July 4th, 1839 and it was dedicated on Nov. 1st 1840.

The reorganized medical faculty was constituted as follows:

B. W. Dudley, M.D.	Anatomy and Surgery.
James C. Cross, M. D.	Institutes of Medicine and Medical Jurisprudence.
John Eberle, M. D.	Theory and Practice of Medicine.
W. H. Richardson, M. D.	Obstetrics and Diseases of Women and Children.
Thomas D. Mitchell, M. D.	Materia Medica and Therapeutics.
Robert Peter, M. D.,	Chemistry and Pharmacy.

James M. Bush, M. D. was adjunct professor of anatomy and surgery. He subsequently became Dr. Dudley's successor in that chair and is hardly less celebrated than his predecessor as a surgeon. Dr. Peter at this time became first connected with the medical department of the University. He was a member of its faculty throughout the remainder of its history and was for many years its Dean, or chief executive officer.

This department maintained its former relative standing comparatively well throughout this period. In 1834-35, it had 255 students while the University of Pennsylvania had 392 and Jefferson Medical College 233. Yale at that time had 44 medical students and Harvard, 82. In 1834, there were 240 in the medical department of Transylvania, which up to Nov. 1838 had had altogether, 3820 students and 1058 graduates. (1).

The Law department of the University was also enlarged in its scope about the time of the reorganizing of its medical faculty and henceforth had three regular professors while its library, increased by the donation of Lexington, Peter (2) tells us, was the finest

(1) Peter's Thoughts on Medical Education in America, p. 12.
(2) History of Fayette County, p. 295.

This department had had, as a rule, only one regular professor since the close of Dr. Holley's administration, but the professors of the school at different times had been such men as John Boyle, Charles Humphreys and Daniel Mayes, while its attendance had ranked up well with similar schools throughout the country. In 1834, Transylvania had one professor and 36 students in its law department; while Harvard had two professors and 32 students; the University of Virginia, one professor and 33 students; Yale two professors and 43 students. In 1839, after its reorganization, Transylvania's Law school had 71 students while Harvard had 120, Yale 45 and the University of Virginia, 72.

The reorganized Transylvania Law faculty (1) was composed of George Robertson, Aaron K. Woolley and Thomas A. Marshall, men rarely if ever excelled in their ability as jurists, or as teachers. They remained in charge of the department throughout the remainder of this period and under them, its attendance and reputation was considerably increased.

About the close of President Cloit's administration, another change in the plan of managing the University was made which marks more emphatically than ever the withdrawal of the state from any

attempt at active participation in its arrangement. By an act approved Feb. 16, 1838, the old trustee system was abolished and the institution was put under the temporary management of five trustees appointed by the governor of the state. On Feb. 20th, 1839, the governing power of the University was vested in a board of eight trustees, two of whom were to be appointed by the Transylvania Institute, three by the City of Lexington, and three by the state legislature, a system of control which was in the main to be retained throughout the remaining history of the institution and which gave to its trustees, now largely local, power to manage it themselves or to transfer its management to other parties, as we shall soon see them doing.

The other members of the Academic faculty at the time of President's Coit's resignation were as follows: Rev. Louis Marshall, D.D. Professor of Ancient Languages; Rev. Robert Davidson, D. D., Professor of Mental and Moral Philosophy; Arthur J. Dumont, L.P., Professor of Mathematics; Robert Peter, M.D., Professor of Natural History and Experimental Philosophy; and Rev. Charles Crow, Principal of the Preparatory department. Dr. Marshall[1] became the acting President of the University and remained so until the beginning of the next regular administration.

The trustees now appear to have endeavored to recall to the aid of the institution an old denominational influence. They attempted to conciliate the Presbyterians, then earnestly striving to make the equipment and endowment of Center College superior to that of Transylvania, by tendering the presidency of the University, Davidson tells us, successively to Dr. J. C. Young, the efficient President of

(1) Dr. Marshall afterwards, in 1850, became the President of Washington College, now Washington & Lee University, Va.

Centre and then to Drs. L. W. Green and R. J. Breckinridge, other ministers of high standing in the Presbyterian Church. These all declined and the position was then offered to Rev. Robert Davidson D.D. also a prominent Presbyterian clergyman. Dr. Davidson who accepted the presidency was a man of considerable reputation and had already for some time occupied a chair in the University faculty. He was inaugurated as President in Nov. 1840, probably at the same time that the large and fine new medical building was dedicated.

The attempt to bring back

Presbyterian support was however, in the main, ineffectual, as, Centre, the distinctively Presbyterian College, had by this time become too firmly established in the affections of the denomination for the effort to be of much avail. Dr. Davidson early recognized this, and as he himself tells us, desparing of being able to stem the tide of general depression now setting in again, and hindered in his work by numerous and vexatious embarrassments, resolved to resign which he did in March 1842.

His resignation may have been hastened by the consumation of negoations, begun perhaps before his election, but not leading to any definite result until after he resigned. As early as 1840, the trustees, whether on their own initiative or not, does not appear, had made overtures to the General Conference of the Methodist Episcopal Church in the United States, looking toward the the control of the University by that body, which, under the circumstances, they probably considered capable of bringing stronger denominational support to the institution than even the Presbyterians. At the meeting of this Conference, held in Baltimore in may 1840, the matter was taken up, and seven commissioners(1) were appointed from the church at large and Kentucky Conference to consider it and to carry out the transfer if it was deemed desirable.

The directing spirit in this movement was Rev. H. B. Bascom, D.D., ... of his denomination and after-

wards, when the division of the church occurred, a Bishop of its southern branch. Dr. Bascom had been, since 1832(1) a prominent professor in Augusta College, an institution long considered the adopted College of Kentucky Methodism under whose auspices it had been mainly founded, but he seems to have been conscientious in thinking that that institution was no longer available for the highest and best educational purposes of his denomination, and therefore devoted himself with his accustomed energy, which was very great, to securing the control of Transylvania University for his church. He experienced considerable opposition from the friends of Augusta, whose funds he vainly tried to secure for the new enterprise; but, after considerable negotiation, was able to effect the desired arrangement. Either because he feared an appeal to the legislature on account of his opposition of Augusta, or because he did not believe such action necessary, no legislative sanction was obtained for the transfer which was made by the trustees on Sept.,21,1841.

(1)For the names of these Commissioners,see Alexander's Earliest Western Schools of Methodism,p372.

(2)This date is given by most all authorities as 1831 but as given as in the text in Henkles Life of Bascom,p. 230,which should all things considered be the most authentic,as also in Spragues Annals,p.6 For a further sketch of Dr. Bascom,see this work. Comprehensive sketches of his life are also to be found in Sprague's Annals,vol.7,pp.,535-538,CollinsHistory of Ky.,vol.I,pp.,453-455. and Smiths History of Ky.,p.,558.

The professional departments still remained on their former basis, the new arrangement applying only to Morrison College, or the academical department, the direct management of which was to be vested in a board of Curators, to be appointed by the General Conference. The Curators were to have control of the department in all important respects, such as the nomination of its faculty, the prescription of its course of study and its internal police and regulation. The church was to be given an additional representation of three members on the board of trustees, which body reserved to itself only a kind of residuary control over the action of the Curators. Kentucky Conference was to be interested in the institution through a visiting Committee of three members to be appointed annually by that body.

The transfer was not regularly ratified by the General Conference until its meeting in 1842, but shortly before that event, in the Spring of that year, Dr. Bascom became, by the appointment of the Conference commissioners, the Acting-President of the University and at once, with characteristic vigor, devoted himself to building up the institution. He associated with himself an able faculty whose personnel in 1843, not long after the beginning of his administration was as follows:

Rev. H. B. Bascom D.D. President and Prof. of Mental and Moral Philosophy, Rev. R. T. P. Allen, A. M. Prof. of Mathematics, Natural Philosophy

and Civil Engineering,Rev.B.H.McCown,A.M.,Prof.of the Ancient Language and Literature,Rev. W.H.Anders n,A.M., Prof. of the English Language and Literature, Rev.J.L.Kemp,A.M.,Adjunct Prof.,of Mathematics,Rev.Thos.H.Lynch, A.M.,Adjunct Prof. of Languages,Rev. Wright Merrick,Prin.Jr.Section Preparatory Department.

Of this faculty Prof. Mc. Cown had like, Dr.Bascom, been long a prominent professor at Augusta and was especially celebrated as a teacher. The faculties of the professional departments of the University were at this time the same as those under the reorganization of 1837, except that Drs.Lothan G.Watson an Leonidas M.Lawson had taken the place of Drs. Eberle and Cross in the medical department.

The new President sat to work with energy and was for a time eminently successful in increasing the patronage of the University, the number of students in its academical department, says Henkle,(1)rising from 20 or 30 at his accession to 251 the second year and 290 the third year of his administration.The professional departments were also well attended.(2)In 1844, Dr. Bascom became

(1)Life of Bascom p.,278.
(2)Catalogues for the years,1842-43,1843-44,1846-47and 1847-48, which have been examined, show that the average annual matriculation in the academical department for these years was 240 of whom something over half were in the preparatory classes.The average annual attendance in the medical department for these years was 215 and the law department,65. In 1843,13 A.B?,30 P.L?, and 59M.D., were conferred.

the regular President, by the appointment of the Curators, who had then been selected for the institution by the General Conference of his church. Under his able management it seemed that Transylvania would soon equal if not excell, in numbers at least, her palmiest days. The partial endowment of the chair of English had been accomplished by 1843. Further endowments were proposed and other ambitious and excellent plans, besides procuring new students, were entertained. Disunion in the church however soon set in and was a great hindrance to the enterprise.

After the division of 1844-45 had taken place in the control of the University passed, in May 1843, into the hands of the Methodist Episcopal Church South. Dr. Bascom was again elected President and in order to secure popularity for the institution had men from all the different parts of the Church elected to its various chairs, but, on account of the irritation and the divided responsibility still remaining in the denomination, especially in Kentucky, neither she nor the South generally increased her support, either in students or funds. So Dr. Bascom discouraged by the situation and despairing of the further enlargement of the institution, resigned in 1849 and soon after steps were taken by his church to abandon the enterprise as a denomination.

Some idea of the standing of Transylvania University in comparison with other institutions in the country may be obtained from

the following statistics of the scholastic year 1842-43. In that year, Harvard had 30 instructors and 245 academic students, while Yale had 30 instructors and 410 academic students Transylvania had 17 instructors and 281 students, a considerable portion of the latter were however doing preparatory work. In the same year Transylvania had 75 law students while Harvard, the only school that exceeded it, had 115. The total number of volumes in the librariesof Harvard and Yale in this year were respectively 53000 and 32200, while there were 12242 volumes in the library of the academical department of Transylvania. Collins tells us in his Sketches(1) that Transylvania in 1847 had libraries numbering 45000 volumes, besides which it had a fine medical museum and an extensive assortment of chemical and philosophical apparatus. Its medical school up to January of that year he tells us had had more than 1500 graduates. Published statements(2) of the yearly expense of attendance at Transylvania at this period show them to have been little less than those of the Eastern Colleges, in fact something more than these of Yale.

(1) Sketches of Ky., p.,236.
(2) In American Almanac and Repository of Useful Knowledge for 1843,tuition at Transylvania was $40, while total College charges were $52, and board, fuel ect. is estimated at $125,(board$100). The same figures for Yale are $33, $54, and $110, (board $70) . The charges for fuel ect. are not given at Harvard but tuition is $75, total College charges $93,and board estimated from $70 to $90, for year.

-Period from 1849 to 1865-

In 1850, the General Conference of the Methodist Episcopal Church South turned over the management of the University to its two conferences in Kentucky, Kentucky and Louisville Conferences, and they not deeming its profession of advantage to themselves, turned it over to the trustees, so that the institution fell back to the plan of control established for it in 1839.

Once more practically abandoned by every one and left to its own slender resources, another season of decline set in in its history, although its collegiate department seems for the next few years to have performed a considerable amount of useful service under the direction of Prof. J.B.Dodd, the Mathematician as acting President, and the professional department continued to have considerable vitality up to the time of the Civil War.

In 1850, the plan of the medical department was changed in such a way as to have its sessions held in the Spring, instead of the fall and Winter as before, and its faculty took the principal part in establishing, to act in conjunction with it, the Kentucky School of medicine, in Louisville. This arrangement however after having been tried for four(I) sessions does not seem to have

(I) The period of the trial of this experiment is usually stated as three years, but the University Catalogue of 1850 and the announcement of the Medical School for 1854 show it to have been four years. There were 92 medical students in 1850 and 53 in 1854,(Spring session). In 1850, there were 125 students in the Academical department and 35 in the law department.

been a success, and so, in 1854, the Transylvania School was changed back to a winter session, although an extra spring session was for a time retained. The Kentucky School of medicine was subsequently continued, in other hands, as another rival institution.

In 1856, the University underwent its last reorganization, as a separate institution. We have a return once more to more direct State control and the advent again of the principle of State patronage. The plan formerly advocated by President Peers was also, revived, and the University was, by an act of March 10, 1856,(I) converted into a State Normal School especially designed to supply well trained teachers for the public schools of the State, a much needed and very commendable object. The school was intended to be an indespensable aid to the common school system, and the cause of public school education in Kentucky had never looked brighter than then. This reorganization of the University was doubtless brought about largely through the persistent agitation of the matter, and the unremitting efforts in that direction, of Rev. Robert J. Breckinridge, D.D.LL.D., State Superintendant of Public Instruction from 1847 to 1853, and an enthusiastic advocate of a State Normal school.

Under the new arrangement State regulation was secured by the appointment of a board of trustees composed of the former trustees and the principal State office. The S''' '''

(I) Collins ''' ''' '''.,'''.,I. '''.,'''.

contribute $12,000 to the enterprise,$7,000 of which was to be used to aid deserving teachers unable to properly educate themselves and $5,000 was to go to the general support of the institution. The grounds and buildings of the University at that time were
(I)
estimated to be worth about $100,000 and its whole property and funds about $200,000, its income from endowment being a little less than $4,000 annually. The institution was not to be converted into a Normal school exclusively but the Normal department was to be made its most p......... , while other regular coll. courses were to be maintained to which the State teachers were to have free access and thus be enabled to greatly broaden their education.

An excellent President was selected for the new school in the person of Rev.L.W.Green D.D. Pres. Green resigned the presidency of Hampden-Sidney College to accept the position. He was a former student of Transylvania University, an alumnus of Centre College in its first graduating class in 1824 and was subsequently a professor there before going to Virginia.

The school was opened auspiciously with 80 students, on Sept.7,1856
(2) and on Nov.12,following, (3) the President was ceremonious-

(I)President Green's Inaugural Address.
(2) Collin's History of Ky.,vol.I,p.73.
(3)Ibid.,vol.,I,p.77.

ly inaugurated under all the old Transylvania forms. The attendance rapidly increased and under the judicious management of Pres. Green excellent progress toward the desired ends was being made, when the legislature, on Feb.13,1858, having previously refused for some reason to renew the appropriation for its support, repealed the act establishing the institution. President Green had already despaired of its success and had resigned in the latter part of 1857. He became the President of Centre College on Jan.1,1858.

So at the end of the two years for which the original appropriation had been made, the Normal School feature of th University was entirely abandoned and the institution reverted to its status prior to the act of 1856. The only reason the writer has seen suggested for the withdrawal of legislative support from the Normal school was that the appropriation made in its behalf encroached on the revenue of the public school fund from which it seems to have been drawn. The State could certainly have advanced the needed amount, and much more, from other sources of revenue, or from direct taxation, and been many times repaid by the results of so doing. Failure to do this lost for her, as it proved, the last practical opportunity of making of Transylvania University a real State institution and causing it to serve an important State purpose, the lack of proper provision for which is still one of the deficiences of her public school system, although that need is considerably supplied by the present Normal department of the State Agricultur-

al and Mechanical College.

After 1858, the University sank hopelessly. Its academic department struggled on for a time under Abram Drake and, during the Civil War, became simply a local grammar school under Prof. J. K. Patterson, the present efficient President of the State College. It lost one of its domitories in 1860 by fire.

The Medical department of the University existed with varying success up to the opening of the Civil War. Its faculty in 1859 was composed of Drs. E.L.Dudley, S.L.Adams, W.S.Chipley, B.P.Drake, S.M.Letcher, H.M.Skillman, J.M.Bush, and Robert Peter. Its building was for a time used as an army hospital and was, on May 22, 1863, destroyed by a fire which also consumed practically all its equipment. the School had had altogether 6406 students of whom 1854 had graduated(I). It has never been resurrected since, on its old basis, but a department of Kentucky University was for a time maintained under a similar name.

The law department had a somewhat similar history during this period, closing its career at the opening of the War. Judge Robertson remained connected with it most, if not all, of the time, and its other professors during this period, were Madison C. Johnson, George B. Kinkead, and Francis K. Hunt. The last three were later connected with Law department of Kentucky University. Judge Robertson

(I)Collins History of Ky. vol. 2, p. 184.

during his long connection with the school, extending for more than twenty years had lectured to more than three thousand young men, over two thousand of whom had graduated.(I).

The libraries and apparatus of all kinds belonging to the University were scattered and much of them destroyed during the war and its prospects were indeed gloomy near the end of that struggle. The trustees had, in 1863, shortly after the acceptance of the gift to the State from the general government made by the Congressional land grant act of 1862, endeavored to have the institution made the foundation of the Agricultural and Mechanical College provided for by that act, but short-sighted policy had prevented the State from then undertaking the establishment of that institution and thus accepting the very advantageous offer made by the trustees of the University.

The outlook for the latter institution had not improved in 1864, when Kentucky University, having lost its building at Harrodsburg by the fire, was looking for a new location. The trustees of Transylvania, then seeing their opportunity to perpetuate the character and usefullness of Lexington as an educational center, proposed to transfer all its property and funds, amounting at that time to about $100000., in real estate and $59000., in endowment, to

(I) Biographical Sketch of Gov. L.W.Powell, p., 23.

Kentucky University, on condition of that institution being located in Lexington and fulfilling all the trusts incumbent under the charter of Transylvania University. Their offer was accepted and the union with Kentucky University consumated by the aid of Legislative action on Jan. 22, 1865.

While the equity of this transfer of what was largely, at least legally, State property to a denominational institution may be questioned by some, it is certainly true that that the property has since been of eminently more educational value to the people of the State at large than it was at the time, or than it seemed likely to be at any time soon. Since Jan.1865, Transylvania University has ceased to exist, as a separate institution, becoming then a part and parcel of Kentucky University with the history of which her history has since blended. The reasons for the failure of Transylvania University, as indicated by the progress of this narrative, are not far a-field, but as they are of some special interest and perhaps in some ways instructive, it may be worth while to recount them somewhat explicitly as follows:-

I, The initial endowment, as in the case of the early academies, was not sufficient to make the institution self-sustaining, nor had the State sufficiently committed herself to the policy of ample regular appropriations, supplementary to the endowment. The State had

not assumed moral or pecuniary obligations sufficently large nor had she committed herself to a policy of sufficiently liberal support through taxation, either or both of which could be plead in behalf of future aid. Unless something of the kind had been done in the early history of the institution through the influence of prominent public men, as was the case later in regard to Jefferson and the University of Virginia, public opinion was not sufficiently strong in its behalf to demand that the University be properly supported.

2, The institution was never made a distinctively State enterprise, as the State had only a partial control over it, being as a rule associated with some form of denominational management. The power of each being just sufficient to hinder thatof the other . Either power by itself might have built up a great University, but together they could not, as it was impossible for them to cooperate harmoniously. Then too the power of each denomination, when attempting to operate the institution, was hampered by the fears and jealousies of the others, as was later the case in regard to Kentucky University, where another attempt was made to build up a great University, with the same union of forces, as in the case of Transylvania origanally, but with these forces reversed in order.

3, This lack of proper cooperation, always in the nature of the case more or less necessary, was rendered much more so in the early history of Kentucky by the prevalence in the State, especially among its public men of French Deistic ideas which naturally

put the religious bodies more on the defensive and made them more sensitive to what they thought were attacks upon their faith when probably there was no intention of anything of the kind. This same feeling seems to have led,at least to a considerable extent,to the educational institutions of the State generally taking such a decided denominational charact r.

4. By reason of the plan of joint control,just described, the University was never placed under the direct supervision of the State authorities who could hold its management responsible and could themselves be called to account. Its board of trustees were in the main,throughout its history, either by law or practice, self-perpetuating,not even having, as a rule, to report their action in any way to any superior officer. The plan of their organization was very similar to that of the early academy boards and gave,as we have seen in the case of these, great opportunity for the creation and perpetuation of factions among themselves, for the carrying out of schemes,denominational or otherwise,and for irresponsible action generally.

The record of Transylvania University,for the two generations which it existed,is in many respects a proud one. Although unusually hampered in its usefulness in many ways,especially by the unfortunate plan of its organization and the state of public opinion on religious and educational questions,never being largely endowed or regularly supported by either State,denomination

or individuals, and always depending largely on tuition fees for its maintenance, it perhaps accomplished as much, or even more, than any other of the earlier educational institutions of this country in the same period counting from the foundation of each. The record of growth and expansion during the Holley era may certainly fairly be said never to have been excelled, if equaled in America, in the same length of time until comparatively recent years. The history of the professional departments was especially brilliant, for a long time almost entirely eclipsing that of any rivals in the West of that day. Its medical faculty with the celebrated Dr. Dudley at its head, for forty years, and, at various times, including such other men, as Cadwell, Cooke, Drake, Short, Yamdell, Cross, Bush, and others, was quite generally unsurpassed of its kind in the country. The faculty of its law college, embracing, at different times, such names as those of Barry, Bledsoe, Boyle, Humphreys, Robertson, Mayes, Marshall, Wooley and others, was almost, if not quite, as noted.

   We have already spoken in a general way of the number of graduates in the various departments. Among the names of those reaching in number into the thousands, are such men as Joseph Stoddard Johnson, Richard M. Johnson, Jefferson Davis, Dr. B.W. Dudley, Thomas F. Marshall, Richard H. Menifee, John Boyle, James Mc. Chord, Dr. Joseph Buchanan, John Rowan, William T. Barry, Jesse Bledsoe, Chas. S. Morehead, Elizah Hise, "Duke" Gwinn, Chas. A. Wickliffe, Robert H. Bishop, Robert J. Breckinridge and a host of others.

thus described by Collins,(I) statesmen,jurists,orators,surgeons, divines, among the greatest in the World's history —men of mark in all the professions and calling of busy life.

Morehead (2) speaks as follows of the work of the institution- an institution which has nursed to maturity the intellect of the commonwealth- having in the progress of sixty years filled her assemblies with law-givers - her cabinets with statesmen- her judicial tribunals with ministers of justice-her pulpits with divines and crowded the professional ranks at home and abroad with ornaments and benefactors of their Country."

One or more of these alumni were to be found, at the close of the University's history, in almost every community of any size in the South and West, where they were principally located, and upon the history of which sections and through them upon that of the whole Country they have exerted a great influence.

(I) History of Ky. vol. 2,p.184.
(2) Boonesborough Address,p.,81.

-Bibliography-

All the Works referred to in regard to the early State University System, except Bradfords Laws, Littell and Swigerts Statutes, Spaldings Early Catholic Missions, Mc Murtri's Sketches and the Report of the Commissioners of 1822, also contain some information about Transylvania University. The following additional authorities have been consulted in regard to the facts of the University's History:--

Sprague's Annals of the American Pulpit.

Henings Statutes at Large.

Sketches of North Carolina by Rev. W.H.Foote, D. D., New York, 1846.

A Tour in Ohio, Indiana and Kentucky in 1805, by Josiah Espy, Cincinnati, 1817.

A History of the Church in Kentucky for Forty Years, Containing the Memoirs of Rev. David Rice, by Robert H. Bishop, Lexington, 1824.

Notes on Kentucky History by John Bradford, published in the Ky., Gazette between Aug.,25, 1823 and Jan.,9,1829.

An Address delivered at Boonesborough in Commemoration of the First Settlement of Kentucky by J.T.Morehead, Frankfort, 1840.

A History of Lexington, Kentucky by George W. Ranck, Cincinnati, 1872.

An Address to the Public in regard to the Controversy about President Holley, by Professors Barry, Bledsoe, Dudley, and Caldwell,

A Discourse on the Genius and character of Rev., Horace Holley, LL.D., (also called Memoirs),by Charles Caldwell, M.D., Boston, 1828.

Autobiography of Charles Caldwell, M.D., edited by Harriot Warner, Philadelphia,1855.

Memoirs of the Life and Services of Daniel Drake, M.D. by E.D. Mansfield,LL.D.,Cincinnati 1855.

Memoirs of Rev. Thomas Cleland, D.D., by E.P. Humphrey and Thomas H. Cleland, Cincinnati, 1859.

The Life of Rev. H.B. Bascom,D.D. LL.D., by Rev., M.M. Henkle, Nashville, 1856.

A Scrap-Book of Law, Politics, Men and Times, by George Robertson, LL.D., Lexington, 1855.

A Biographical Sketch of Hon. L.W. Powell, by direction of the General Assembly, Frankfort, 1868.

Thoughts on Medical Education in America, by Robert Peter, M.D., Lexington, 1838.

Thoughts on Public Education in America, by Robert Peter, M.D., Frankfort, 1877.

The Minutes of the Board of Trustees of Transylvania University. These are preserved in the Archives of Kentucky University and are quite complete up to Feb.1818, after which date they are quite fragmentary.

By-Laws of Transylvania University, Lexington,1818.

Inaugural Address of President Woods, Lexington, 1828.

Laws of Transylvania University, Lexington, 1820.

The Transylvania Journal of Medicine for Oct., Nov., and Dec.,1831.

Inaugural address of President Peers, Lexington,1833.

Extra of the Lexington Intelligence for April 11, 1837.

Statutes of Transylvania University, Lexington, 1842.

 A Communication from the Commissioners of Kentucky Conference to the Legislature of Kentucky in reply to a Memorial from the Trustees of Augusta College, Lexington, 1843.

The Transylvania Journal of Medicine for December, 1850.

Inaugural Address of President Green, Frankfort, 1856.

Reports of the State Superintendent of Public Instruction, from 1839 to 1857, and Appendix to the Report of 1875-76.

Niles Weekly Regirter, September 1811-July 1849, 3rd., Edition, 72 vols., Baltimore, Washington and Philadelphia,1811-1849.

The American Almanac and Repository of Useful Knowledge, 1830-1861, 32 vols., Boston and New York,1830-61.

 The last two Authorities have been consulted mainly for the statistics used, which,in the case of Transylvania, have been fully verified by reference to a number of old Catalogues. The History of Transylvania University by Robert Peter M.D.,edited by Johanna Peter, Louisville,1896,has been carefully examined, but,as this chapter had been practically Completed before it was accessible,very

and his second subordinate Philosophy. At intervals between 1 ?? and 1??, he has collected, mainly on the ground, the facts for the accompanying dissertation on the History of Education in ??.

May 2, 1900.

www.ingramcontent.com/pod-product-compliance
Lightning Source LLC
Chambersburg PA
CBHW032113230426
43672CB00009B/1723